CANOEING
Safety & Rescue

Doug McKown

Acknowledgments
I would like to express my gratitude to all those who provided assistance, encouragement, and their own knowledge and experience in the development of this book. For their special efforts in taking, or appearing in photographs, I would like to thank the following: my wife Donna, Jack & Eileen McKown, Jim Buckingham, Pam Little, Bill & Lynn Calvert, Heather Dempsey, Keith Webb and Keith Morton who edited the manuscript.

3rd printing 2001

Printed and bound in Canada by
Hignell Printing Limited, Winnipeg

We acknowledge the financial support of the Government of Canada through the Book Publishing Industry Development Program (BPIDP) for our publishing activities.

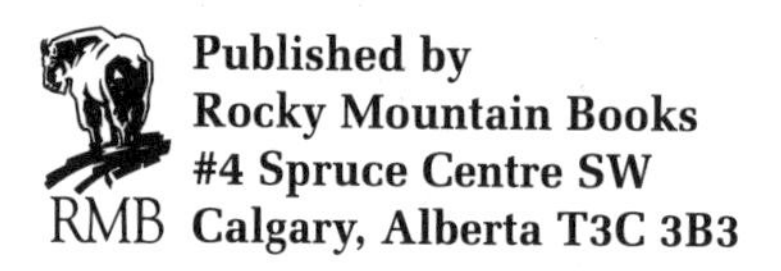
RMB
Published by
Rocky Mountain Books
#4 Spruce Centre SW
Calgary, Alberta T3C 3B3

Canadian Cataloguing in Publication Data

McKown, Doug, 1953-
Canoeing safety and rescue

Includes index
ISBN 0-921102-11-9
1. Canoes and canoeing--Safety measures.
2. Rescue work. I. Title.
GV783.M24 1992 797.1'22'0289 C92-091472-1

Contents

Introduction - 5

Safety & Rescue Equipment - 9

Planning for a Safe Trip - 29

The Rescue Plan - 51

Rescue Skills &Techniques - 59

Rigging & Pulling Systems - 85

First Aid & Evacuation - 113

Checklists - 122

First Aid Supplies - 122 Survival Kit - 123
Equipment Checklist - 12 Ground to Air Signals - 124
What to Do after a Capsize - 125
Flowchart of the Ten Steps to Rescue - 126
Flowchart for Choosing a Rescue Method - 127

Index - 128

Introduction

One of the great attractions of canoeing is the personal, independent nature of the sport. I always feel a great satisfaction in being able to travel almost effortlessly with little more than a canoe and a paddle.

However, the very independence provided by the canoe, and the remoteness of the places to which it can take one, puts the responsibility for safety and rescue directly on the individual paddler. You are on your own, and the outcome of an emergency will depend entirely on your own resources and resourcefulness.

Problems and accidents that develop in canoeing can happen quickly, when you least expect them, demanding immediate response. Rarely are there professional rescue personnel available to assist soon enough, so canoeists must be able to help themselves.

A group of my paddling friends found out how fast problems can develop one stormy afternoon, during a wilderness tour on a northern Canadian lake. The weather had been unsettled all day, with occasional small rain squalls passing through. It was late afternoon, and three canoes were paddling through some scattered islands on a vast lake. Very quickly, the group became engulfed by a fierce squall. The weather grew more violent than the canoeists had anticipated, and in minutes the strong winds generated steep, choppy waves on the relatively shallow lake. All the canoeists tried to head for shore in the face of horizontal driving rain. The bowsman of the third canoe was shocked when he saw the sternsman's paddle in the canoe ahead snap cleanly in half. Before the paddlers had a chance to react, the canoe broached, and a large breaking wave crashed over the canoe, swamping it. The paddlers in the third canoe looked on in horror as their friends were plunged into the freezing cold water.

What would you do? How would you react to this kind of emergency? Fortunately, these paddlers were well prepared and were able to handle the incident themselves. They had a plan, and they had the skills to carry out the plan. All the paddlers and the equipment were brought quickly and safely to shore, and this episode remained an interesting but harmless event during a successful canoe trip.

Canoeing provides a satisfying physical activity which can meet the needs of almost anyone. It is an activity that can be enjoyed at any level of skill, or athletic ability. However, it is this very broad range of participation which makes safety and rescue such a difficult, but important aspect of canoeing.

Unfortunately, as in other sports, proficiency and experience in canoeing skills does not automatically imply proficiency in safety procedures. I've met a great many paddlers who have numerous years of canoe tripping experience, and yet are totally unfamiliar with the basics of canoe safety, and with rescue techniques.

Canoeing is normally a very safe sport, but it does have inherent dangers, and accidents do happen. However, the fact that there are risks associated with the sport is no reason for anyone to avoid canoeing. There is nothing more dangerous on this earth than getting into an automobile and going out to travel on our highways, yet people do this every day of their lives without a second thought. I know that if I had a choice, I'd always prefer to take my kids canoeing, rather than let them get into a car.

Accidents, by definition, are unexpected events which occur as a result of unforeseen circumstances. However, most of your canoeing accidents will be small ones, and should remain small if you plan your trip well, operate safely, and have the appropriate skills and abilities to deal with emergencies.

Safety and **Rescue** are two entirely different concepts. Safe canoeing is much more a state of mind than any specific physical activity, while rescue is something which requires a wide repertoire of skills and access to suitable equipment. Safety is the philosophy of accident prevention. It is a process of planning, assessing risks, and operating in a way which minimizes the chance of an accident occurring. Rescue, on the other hand, is the concept of accident survival. This is the process of dealing with an incident, or emergency, in such a way as to ensure that the situation is brought under control and that no further injury or damage occurs.

Because you will be involved in canoe accidents very infrequently, it can be difficult to maintain a high level of proficiency in your rescue skills. Practise in these skills must be ongoing on a regular basis. Practise sessions should be conducted in conditions which are as similar as possible to a real life situation. This means extreme care must be taken to ensure that the training sessions are safe for all participants. Training sites can provide all the dangers and hazards of a real life rescue. They can actually be more dangerous since this is the time when paddlers are learning new skills and experimenting with new techniques.

The more that you practise rescue skills, the more safety awareness you will acquire. As you increase your skills and experience, you will develop safe canoeing habits that you can apply in all your paddling activities. Canoeing is a great sport, and safe canoeing habits are easy to develop. If you become a safe canoeist, you will have a much better chance of becoming an old canoeist.

Disclaimer
Many of the safety and rescue techniques described in this book are intended for use in specific circumstances and may be hazardous if applied inappropriately by unskilled or insufficiently trained paddlers. The onus is on the reader to apply the techniques described appropriately and correctly. These techniques are best learned and practised under the guidance of a qualified instructor.

1

Safety & Rescue Equipment

Your ability to provide an effective rescue, and even your own survival, depends on the equipment that you have with you at the time of the accident. On a paddling trip you must make do with what you can carry in your canoe, so planning for rescue includes deciding what equipment and how much of it to take with you. Because you can only carry a limited amount, you should plan to carry the most versatile selection of equipment to allow you as many options as possible in an emergency.

How Much Safety and Rescue Equipment Should You Carry ?

In order to deal with a canoeing emergency you must have the required rescue equipment actually with you at the time of the accident. I am the kind of person who carries just about the same amount of supplies with me for a two hour trip, as I do for a two or three day expedition. If I don't think a capsize is likely, I only carry one spare set of clothes. If mores spills are possible, then I either carry more spare clothes, or I wear a wetsuit or drysuit to keep warm.

In addition to spare clothes, I also carry rain gear, first aid kit, repair kit, rescue gear, food, matches, a tarp or bivy sac for emergency shelter, and my survival kit on my person at all times. Each canoe should be as self contained as possible with respect to safety and rescue gear, in case you become separated from the rest of the group. The better prepared individual paddlers are for rescue, the more successful the entire group will be in dealing with any emergency.

Keeping Equipment Waterproofed

Any gear that you carry in your canoe must be in a completely waterproofed container if it is going to be of any use to you. There are many waterproof bags on the market, designed specifically for canoeing, and they are available in many different sizes. However, a sturdy pack with two heavy duty plastic garbage bags inside works just as well providing the bags are securely sealed. To create an effective seal, put one plastic bag inside the other, lining the pack, and load your gear. Squeeze down on the plastic bag to ensure that you have removed as much air as possible, tightly twist the end of the bag, fold it over on itself, and tie it securely with a piece of string. Seal both of the bags individually and your gear will stay dry even during a long swim.

Two large plastic bags, individually sealed inside a pack, will keep all your gear dry.

Specially designed waterproof packs and containers come in may different sizes and shapes.

Dressing for Safety

The clothing you wear must be sufficient to protect you from the weather while you are paddling, and from the water if you capsize. While the type of clothing needed will vary depending on the climate, the primary concern is warmth.

Paddling Clothing

To keep you warm, clothing must perform three functions. It must keep you dry, insulate your body, and protect you from the wind. Modern fabrics used for making warm outdoor clothing, such as fleece pile, and polypropylene, are excellent for canoeing. These fabrics do not absorb water very easily, and will keep you warm even after they get wet. They not only keep you warm while you are paddling, but also if you are swimming. Because they do not absorb water very well, they also dry out very quickly after a capsize. A warm insulating layer of clothing, in combination with a windproof, and water repellent shell, such as a nylon or Gore-Tex anorak should allow you to paddle comfortably in cool or unpleasant weather and provide some insulation if you capsize.

Wetsuit

If the water is very cold, or if there is a chance of numerous capsizes, then more protection may be in order. Wearing a wetsuit is one way to provide extra insulation. Most paddling wetsuits are made from 3-4 mm neoprene rubber, with a tough nylon coating bonded to both sides. The most popular style is a two piece suit, with one piece in the form of sleeveless coveralls, and a long sleeve jacket to provide full protection. This two piece combination provides the greatest versatility for paddling comfort.

Another popular choice for paddlers is a "shorty" wetsuit. This is a short sleeved, short pants wetsuit, which is less restricting to movement than the long sleeve/leg style.

A wetsuit does not keep you dry. A wet suit functions by trapping a thin layer of water between the rubber of the suit, and

A two-piece wetsuit provides a great deal of versatility for canoeing.

A "shorty" wetsuit is another good compromise for paddling comfort and warmth.

your skin. Your body warms up this layer of water, and allows you to stay warm. To function properly, that is to maintain a thin layer of water up against your skin, the wetsuit must fit snugly over your entire body. A loose fitting wetsuit allows too much water to circulate against your skin and will not perform effectively. Because of the need to fit snugly, many paddlers find a wetsuit to be very confining and too uncomfortable to paddle in for any length of time. Wet suits are also less efficient for paddlers who may be in and out of the water a number of times. Every time you get out of the water, the layer of water inside the wetsuit drains away. When you enter the water again, there is a another inflow of cold water which your body must initially warm up. For these reasons many paddlers prefer to use a drysuit to stay warm.

Drysuit

Drysuits designed for paddling can be one or two piece suits. They are constructed of nylon material which has a completely waterproof coating on the inside surface of the cloth. The neck, wrists and ankles have soft rubber gussets which provide a totally waterproof seal. These seals are vulnerable to snagging unless covered with an outer cuff, and are easily degraded by suntan oil, insect repellent and sunlight. The drysuit, which should be loose fitting to accommodate your own clothing underneath, functions by keeping your clothing dry, and therefore maintaining the clothing's insulating ability. Because they fit loosely, drysuits are quite comfortable to wear, and also allow you to change the amount of insulating clothing you wear underneath, according to the current weather and water conditions. Drysuits also keep you warmer than a wetsuit if you are in and out of the water frequently, because your skin never actually gets wet. They also work better to protect you and keep you warm during rainy weather then does a wetsuit.

One-piece suits with front zippers are easier to get into and out of than rear zipper models and two-piece suits.

Although a wetsuit or drysuit will do the best job of keeping you warm after you capsize, any clothing will help. When you are in the water, clothing helps to reduce the amount of water circulation up against your skin and will always keep you much warmer than no clothing at all.

It is important to keep in mind that you must be prepared for a capsize. No amount of clothing, or a wetsuit, or a drysuit is going to do you any good if you are not wearing it at the time of the capsize. When you are paddling in an area where the water is very cold, but the air temperature is quite warm, it may be tempting to take off the protective wear to increase paddling comfort. Paddlers must always think of the consequences of a capsize in these situations.

Less constricting than a wetsuit, drysuits are becoming more and more popular as they keep you both warm and dry at the same time.

Footwear

Protective footwear is essential for all types of paddling. Footwear must provide both warmth and physical protection for your feet in case you have to walk out, or chase a lost canoe. Shoes for paddling should have secure fastenings which will hold the shoe firmly in place while you are swimming. I prefer the old fashion canvas high-top sneakers, which lace up around the top of your ankle.

Because paddlers feet tend to be wet most of the time, warmth is an important consideration in footwear. The best way to keep your feet warm is to wear either wetsuit socks, or wetsuit boots. Wetsuit socks are made out of the same material as a full wetsuit. They are usually neoprene with nylon on both sides, although some may have nylon on only one side. The nylon on both sides just provides a stronger, more durable material. I prefer wetsuit socks, or neoprene socks as they are also known, since they can usually be worn in place of regular socks inside your normal paddling shoes. Using this combination, the shoe provides physical protection for your foot, while the neoprene sock keeps them warm.

The best wetsuit boots for paddling are the type that are designed for windsurfing. They are a complete, high-top boot made out of neoprene. There is usually a zipper to hold them in place. The important concern about wetsuit boots is to choose a style which has a firm, solid sole which will provide adequate protection for your feet.

You may wish to treat yourself to stretch Gore-Tex socks. Great for touring as they keep your feet dry without your getting foot rot on a long trip.

Headgear

Wearing a helmet is imperative whenever you are paddling closed canoes, such as a C-2 or C-1 on a river, where the objective is to stay in the canoe after a capsize and perform an Eskimo roll. Wearing a helmet is also a wise precaution when you are paddling a canoe which is fitted with thigh straps, or a spray deck, which may hinder a quick exit from the canoe after a capsize.

A wide-brimmed hat helps cut glare to enable you to see better in rapids. A pile, fleece or neoprene cap is good for warmth (remember large amounts of heat are lost through the head).

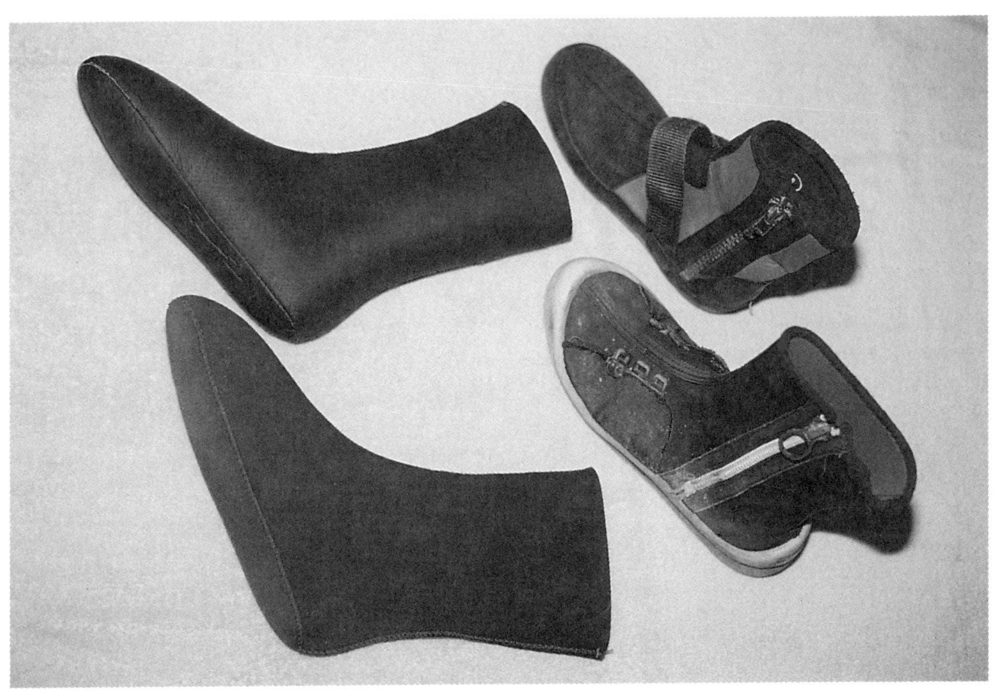

Wetsuit booties and wetsuit socks will keep your feet warm

Personal Flotation Device (PFD'S)

A personal flotation device (PFD) is the most important item of equipment for safe canoeing. One of the most common reasons for water related deaths is that people were not wearing a PFD.

Regulations

The laws and regulations which control the use of PFD'S vary from place to place. Some areas require that you wear the PFD at all times, while others simply require you to have the PFD in the canoe with you. However, to be of any practical use, your PFD must be worn at all times. Planning to put your PFD on after you have capsized is a completely unacceptable option. You will be unlikely to even find your PFD, let alone be able to put it on once you are in the water.

To be legally acceptable, a PFD must be approved by the government. In Canada this will be the Ministry of Transport (MOT), and in the United States it will be the US Coast Guard. A legally acceptable PFD will have a tag inside which indicates this approval.

If you are purchasing a new PFD, you should be careful, as there are many PFD's on the market which are not government approved. It is also true that PFD's which are approved by the US Coastguard are not necessarily legal in Canada, and vice versa. This does not mean they are not good PFD's, they are just not legally accepted by the authorities, often because the manufacturer has not gone to the expense and work of obtaining approval.

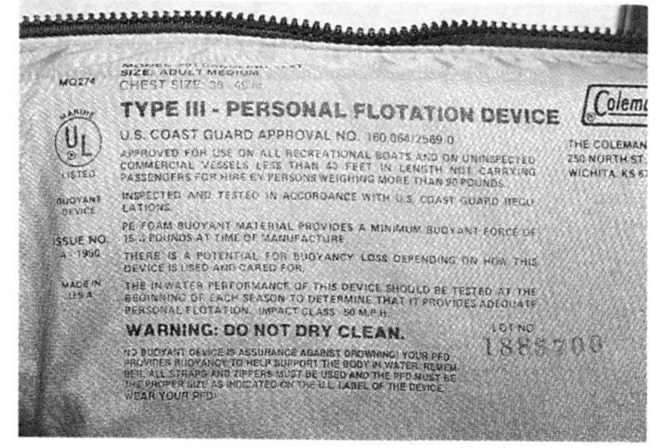

All legally acceptable PFD's will have a label of approval inside.

A Personal Flotation Device is your basic tool for safe canoeing.

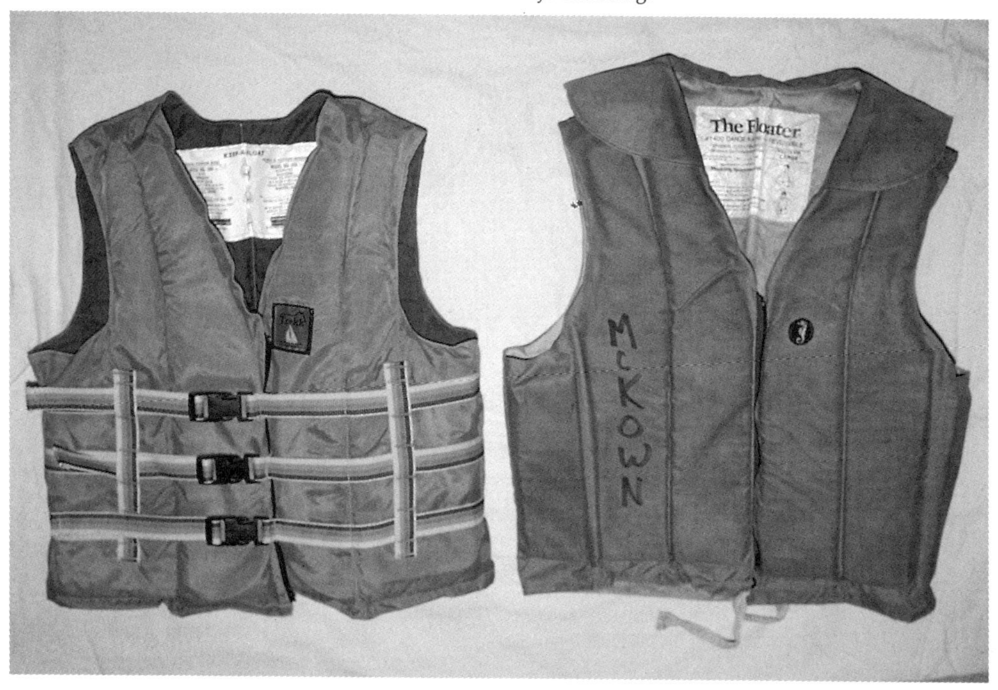

Can I Modify my PFD?

While there are many well designed PFD's on the market today, many paddlers choose to make custom modifications to their own PFD to create one that better suits their individual needs. It is worthwhile to note that any modifications you make to your PFD will void the government approval, but may greatly enhance your personal safety while paddling. It is up to you to decide whether it is more important for you to be within the law or to have a more effective PFD. In some areas, authorities have been known to issue tickets for attaching a knife to the PFD, even though many PFD'S have attachment points for that very purpose!

Buying a PFD

A major consideration in choosing an appropriate PFD is proper fit. You will wear your PFD for long periods of time, and proper fit is important for comfort. If it isn't comfortable, you'll find yourself not wearing it. Also important is the fact that an ill fitting PFD will not do its job. If it is too small, the fasteners cannot be done up properly, and if it is too big it can easily come off in the water even if the fasteners are done up completely. An improperly fitting PFD can also seriously hamper your swimming ability by floating up around your head, interfering with your vision, and hampering the movement of your arms.

A PFD is a compromise between form and function. PFD'S must maximize the amount of flotation, yet still provide as much freedom of movement as possible. Most of the vest style PFD's available have a zipper or clips to hold the front together. These allow for convenient access and are quite secure when properly fastened. Unfortunately this style of PFD tends not to get fastened properly; people leave them open, and zippers slide open unnoticed, or break, and they are so easily removed they tend to get left off.

You can buy vest style PFD's with no front opening. These are pulled on over you head like a sweater, and there are no zippers or clips to break or be left undone. These are usually short, snugly fitting PFD's, designed for paddling closed canoes and kayaks. Because these types of PFD are more difficult to take off and on, once they are on, they tend to stay on. Whenever I purchase a new PFD for canoeing, one of the modifications that I make is to take the zipper out and sew up the front of the vest. That way I can never leave it unfastened, and I don't worry about the closures breaking or coming loose.

After you purchase a new PFD you should become familiar with how it feels in the water. The best thing to do is go to your local pool or lake, put the PFD on, and jump in the water. A PFD fits completely differently in the water than it does on land. This is the time to find out how you float with your PFD on, and how best to swim with it on. During a real emergency, with cold water and dangerous conditions, is not the time to find out that a particular style of PFD doesn't suit you.

I once had a pupil in a canoe course who was wearing a PFD that they had owned for many months, but had never tested, out in the water. When they eventually capsized into a rapid, the PFD floated up high around their neck, limiting their vision and hampering their ability to swim. The victim of this event became quite panicky, and almost caused a serious incident.

This problem of a PFD floating up high on your shoulders can be serious. In fact, if you are unconscious, it is quite possible for many types of PFD's to come off over your head. The addition of a "beaver tail" to your PFD can help to solve this problem. A beaver tail is a strap or piece of material attached to the back of your PFD at the bottom. When you have the PFD on, this strap comes between your legs and is fastened by a quick release buckle or velcro at the front. This holds the PFD in place and makes swimming much easier. It also removes any possibility of the PFD coming off if the paddler is unconscious.

Whatever type of PFD you buy, and whatever modifications you make, the important thing is that you have one and that you wear it. If you are not wearing it when the accident occurs, it is usually far too late. Wearing your PFD and ensuring that all members of the group are wearing theirs is probably one of the most important aspects of safe canoeing.

Carrying a Personal Survival Kit

If you are going to paddle in a remote area, it is imperative that you carry a personal survival kit. This is a kit that is carried **on your person at all times** and is completely separate from, and in addition to, the rest of your gear.

It is not uncommon for paddlers to become separated from their gear and their canoe during an accident. When you finally drag yourself onto the shore after a long cold swim, with nothing available but your freezing wet clothes, a small survival kit can make a big difference to your comfort and possibly to your survival.

A survival kit of this nature must be kept small so that it can be easily carried. If it is too big and bulky, you will tend to leave it at home. If this happens, the kit will survive quite well, but **you** may not be so lucky. How much you choose to carry in your survival kit is up to you.

Some of the basic items are; matches in a waterproof container (or a lighter), candle, fish hooks and line, space blanket, compass, extra heavy-duty aluminum foil, wire saw, snare wire, and emergency food such as soup packets, chocolate, and beef jerky.

Depending on the size of the kit you are willing to carry, you may also include; maps, signalling mirror, whistle, more food, tent fly, insect repellent, water purification tablets, and first aid supplies. A survival kit must be waterproof. Mine stays tightly sealed in a ziplock plastic bag, inside a small nylon pouch which I keep in a specially designed pocket on the inside of my personal flotation device. Be careful that hard articles in the kit do not perforate the bag as damp, beef jerky or moldy dried soup are not too palatable! Wrap softer articles around them for cushioning, or else use a small plastic box lined with a ziplock bag. Use an elastic band to jam the lighter valve closed until needed. A survival kit can also be easily carried in a small belt bag or fanny pack.

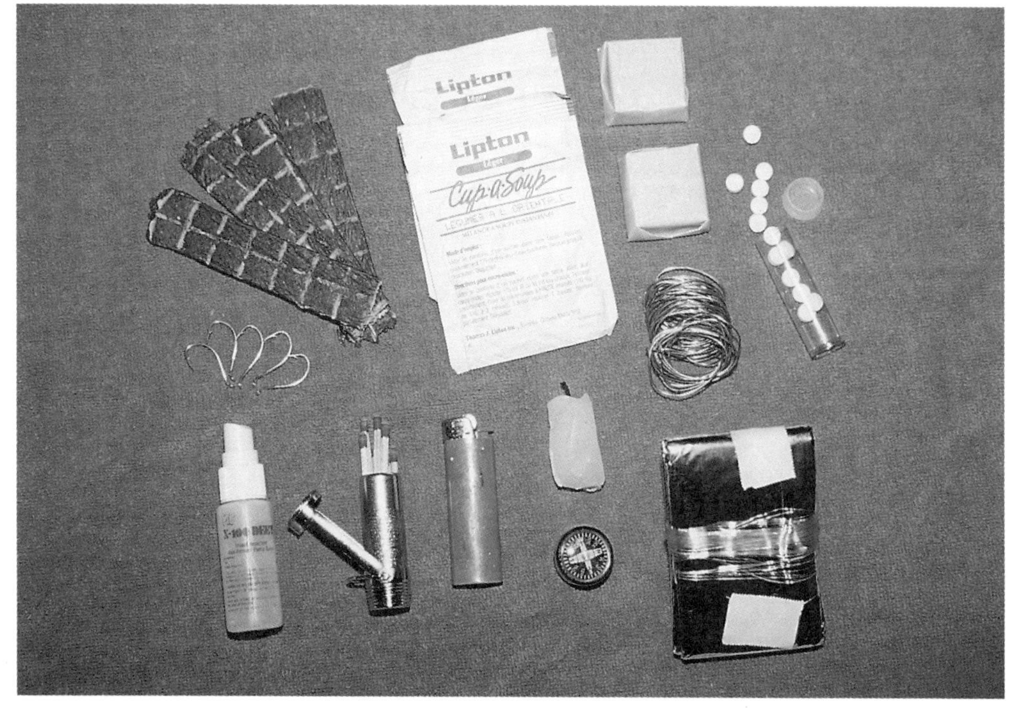

A personal survival kit containing: lighter, candle, compass, fish hooks, beef jerky, chocolate, dry soup, snare wire, water purification tablets, insect repellent, emergency space blanket, aluminum foil, fishing line, waterproof matches.

A Knife for Rescue

All paddlers should carry a knife. Canoe rescues tend to require lots of rope, and the chance of entanglement always exists when paddlers and rope are in the water at the same time. There is also the possibility of PFD's, clothing, and other gear becoming caught on trees and other obstacles and needing to be cut free. You won't often need to use a knife in a hurry, but when the situation does arise, nothing but a readily accessible knife will do the job.

I have been involved in a number of situations where I have had to cut clothing and ropes to effect a rescue. One memorable occasion happened a few years ago while I was teaching a river canoeing course.

One of the student canoes missed an eddy turn, hit a large roller broadside, and capsized. All our students knew the drill for capsizing and the victims, Jim and Sue, were prepared for the rescue procedure. One of our instructors threw a rescue rope, and Jim managed to grab it. However, due to the rough shoreline and powerful current, Jim was unable to maintain his grip on the rope and the canoe. He released the canoe, and was pulled safely to shore. Sue and the canoe floated off down the rapid. At that point all of the other students were safely parked, so I paddled out solo to continue the rescue. I grabbed on to the loose canoe, and had Sue move to the end of my canoe and hold on. We were in the middle of a "busy" grade three rapid. This was not a spot I would normally have chosen to attempt the type of rescue known as a T-rescue, but Sue was very cold by now. I knew this particular stretch of river very well. If I could execute the T-rescue quickly, it would be the safest and fastest method of dealing with the situation. I turned the swamped canoe over and hauled it up and across the gunnels of my canoe.

That was the moment when everything went wrong. I had the canoe three quarters of the way across when it stuck fast. I couldn't pull it any further across, and I couldn't lift it or flip it over. What had happened, was that a large day pack had been tied to the canoe thwart, and was now jammed up against the side of my canoe. Contrary to the instructors' directions, Jim and Sue had tied this pack directly to the thwart, instead of leaving some free rope which would have allowed for a T-rescue.

Meanwhile, Sue and I were still bouncing and swirling down the rapid. My only choice at this point, was to cut the pack free of the canoe. Holding on to the rescued canoe with one hand, I reached for the knife which lives in a quick release sheath sewn on the front of my PFD. To my horror the knife wasn't there, the sheath was empty. I remembered that when we had stopped for lunch about an hour previous to the accident my knife was the one used to slice the tomatoes for the sandwiches. Somehow, at the end of the lunch break, my

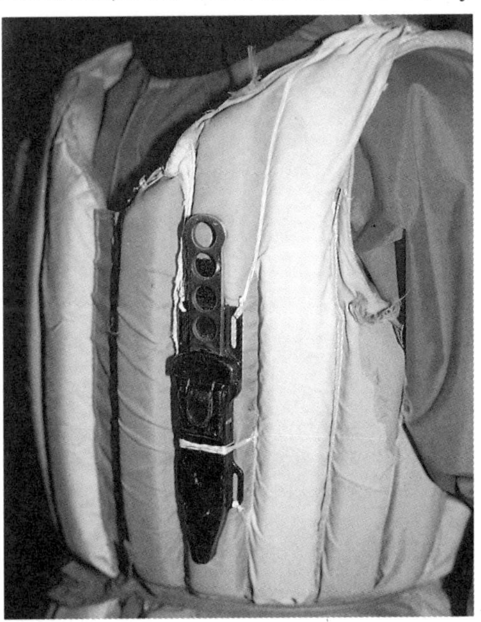

A knife should always be immediately available to the paddler. Some paddlers prefer to mount the knife handle down, but I have found the up-position to be more secure and just as readily accessible.

knife had been packed away with the other supplies instead of being returned to my sheath. Now, here I was in the middle of a rapid trying to perform a rescue, with a simple but serious problem to solve, and my knife was gone. This oversight turned an otherwise simple rescue into a much longer bumping, twisting ride down a long rapid before I was able to get Sue and the canoe safely to shore. The lesson to be learned from the above story is that the knife must be instantly accessible at all times. A knife in a sheath on your waist, under your jacket and PFD, is not really accessible. Nor is a folding knife in your pocket, or worse still, inside a drysuit or pack. Many paddlers have found that the best place to carry a knife is to have it fixed to the outside of their PFD. Because the PFD is always worn, on the outside of clothing, the knife is always readily accessible. You don't need an expensive or fancy knife. For years I used a small sheath knife costing about $5 from a local sporting goods store. I sewed the sheath to the chest of my PFD, and used velcro to hold the handle of the knife in place. This fastening was very secure and lasted for quite a few years. For the more adventurous, there are plenty of fancy knives available with spring loaded sheaths and quick release buttons.

Carry a Signalling Device

A whistle is another vitally important item for paddlers to carry. It is actually required by small craft safety regulations in many jurisdictions to be carried as a "noisemaking device". In any emergency, communications are usually critical to the success of the rescue. While many paddlers have a system of visual signals that they use, visual signals are only going to work if the intended receiver is looking in the direction of the signal. Audio signals on the other hand are especially useful for gaining peoples' attention, and can alert many paddlers at once. They can also function well at night or when the other party is out of visual contact. A whistle can be used by a victim who has capsized, lost his paddle, and needs to alert the rest of the group to his problem. Whistles are inexpensive and, worn on a string attached to your PFD, can be ready for instant use. Be sure to buy a waterproof whistle. No whistle will work when it is full of water, but any whistle for use while paddling must be able to be sounded after a dunking and a quick shake .

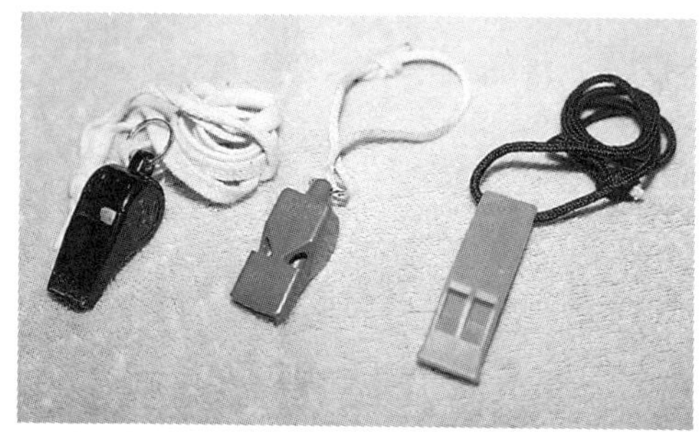

A whistle is always handy for getting the attention of other paddlers.

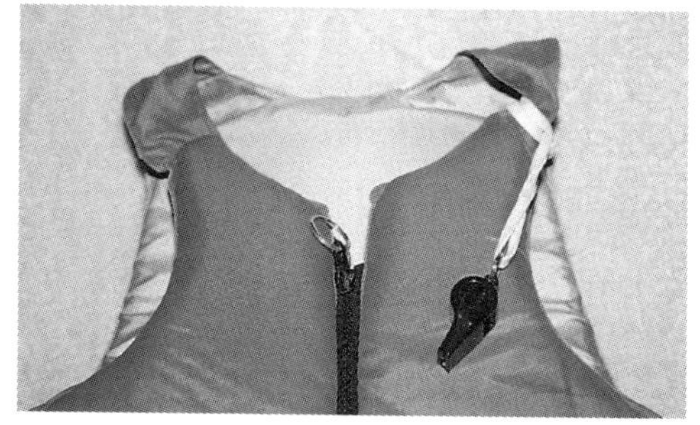

Carried on your PFD, the whistle is always ready for instant use.

There are other signalling devices which can also be of use to paddlers during a rescue. A simple metal signalling mirror works very well to signal searchers or rescuers on the ground, as well as being handy for alerting aircraft.

A small flare gun can also be very useful for gaining attention. These are entirely portable, and can be carried in any emergency kit. Flare guns work quite well in attracting the attention of ground rescuers or aircraft, especially at night or in low light conditions.

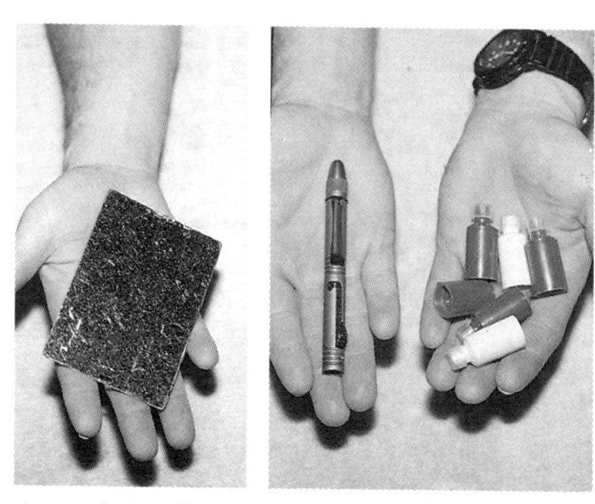

A metal signalling mirror (left) is a handy device for gaining the attention of rescuers. A small flare gun can easily be carried in any emergency kit.

Carry a Bailer

A bailer is legally required by most small craft safety regulations for the simple reason that it is an important and practical safety tool. It allows you to keep your canoe empty, without the necessity of going to shore and overturning the canoe. On lakes it is not uncommon to be taking on small amounts of water if the weather causes rough conditions. With a fully loaded canoe, it can be quite bothersome to go ashore, unload the canoe and empty it. This may lead to paddlers waiting too long before going ashore to empty, and consequently becoming swamped by an unexpected wave which would have been no problem to a dry canoe. Rocky shores or waves may preclude landing and emptying until it is too late. If there is one canoe in a group without a bailer, it may have to go ashore a number of times, possibly causing the group to become separated.

I learned to appreciate the need for carrying a bailer during a canoe trip in the mountains of British Columbia. This was about fifteen years ago while I was looking after a group of teenagers on a lake canoe trip. There were two adult leaders in charge of our little expedition, and myself, the only other adult, in charge of about fifteen kids. Our problem arose when the decision was made to paddle across a large mountain lake. It was the middle of the afternoon, and the weather was pleasant with a light breeze blowing. These kids were all beginner paddlers with reasonably full loads in their canoes for our week long trip. I had some initial misgivings in the back of my mind about the crossing. The lake was about one kilometre wide, and we were planning to travel across at a slight diagonal. The water was very cold, and I knew how fast and violently the wind could come up in this area. Sure enough, not long after we embarked, a very strong wind developed, creating large, white capped waves. It was a directly following wind. Since the kids would have had a very difficult time turning their canoes around and paddling back against the wind, we decided the safest option was to try and continue on our planned route. It wasn't until that particular moment that I realized there were no bailers in any of our canoes. Our problem was slowly but inexorably developing. Almost every one of the large following waves slopped over the gunnels virtually unnoticed, but deposited a splash of water into the canoe. The occasional bigger wave brought in even more. Eventually the kids' canoes were getting heavier and heavier, and more difficult to control. The heavier and slower the canoes became, the more water was taken on. The trip leaders were obviously worried, and the kids were becoming fearful. I was already having visions of disaster; fifteen kids swimming and screaming in a windy wavy freezing lake. However, lady luck stepped in once again and we managed to reach the far shore before anyone actually swamped. We had eighteen very shaken, tired, but wiser canoeists.

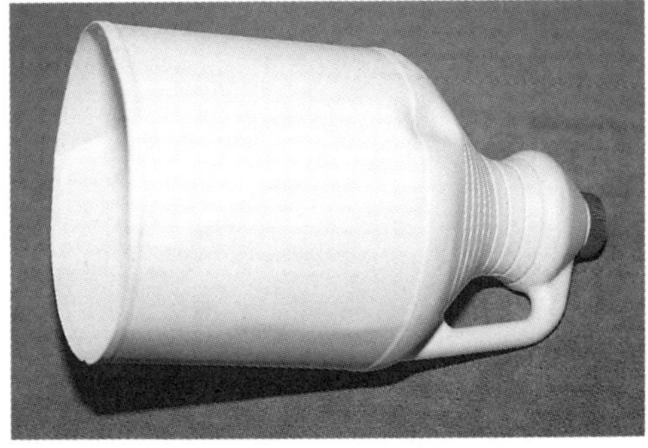

Bailers are a simple but useful tool for safe canoeing.

Bailers are simple to make. After long years of experimentation with many different materials, I have found that nothing works better than the old white plastic, "Javex" type bottle. Cut off the bottom quarter of the bottle, and you have a perfect bailing device. The round style bottles are preferable to the square ones. They form better to the shape of the hull as you scoop out the water. The moulded plastic handle provides a convenient point of attachment to secure it to your canoe by means of a rope, sling, or carabiner. It can also be helpful to permanently glue the top onto the bottle, as it can work loose over time and become lost just when you need it the most.

Rope

Rope is a prime tool for rescues in and around canoes. Ropes are used for painters, end loops, tying in gear, for anchor lines, pulling systems, river crossing, lashing together and stabilizing canoes. There are many different types of rope available for many different purposes.

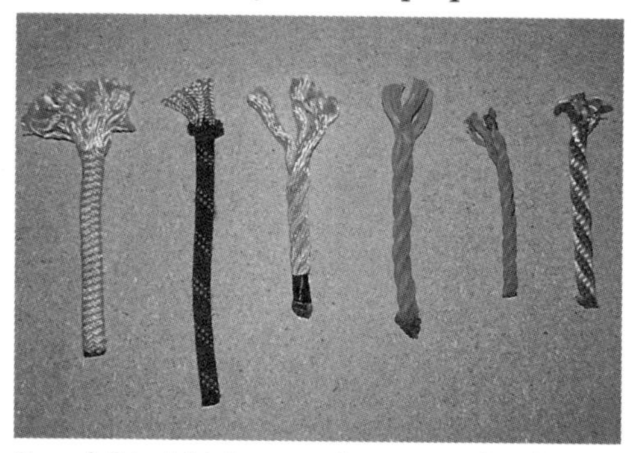

From left to right: kernmantle marine nylon, kernmantle perlon mountaineering rope, 11 mm laid marine nylon, 11 mm laid polypropylene, 8 mm laid polypropylene, 11 mm braided polypropylene.

When used for any activities where people may be in the water with the rope, such as for painters, tow ropes, throwbags, or tie-in ropes, it is very important that the rope floats. A floating rope is more visible and because it is on the surface it is less likely to cause entanglement problems with people or obstructions.

Polypropylene

Polypropylene is the most commonly used material for floating ropes. The standard yellow laid (twisted) polypropylene rope is inexpensive, readily available, and eminently suitable for many purposes. 9.5 mm polypropylene has a breaking strength 1000 kg, and 12.2 mm has a breaking strength of 1600 kg. As the recommended working range for a rope is about 10% of its breaking strength, 9.5 mm polypropylene can be used with confidence for loads of around 100 kg. This is quite sufficient for use in throwbags, securing gear in a canoe, or for general lashing and tying.

One of the main advantages of polypropylene rope is that it does not absorb water at all, remaining light and drying quickly. This "dry" quality of polypropylene also prevents the rope from freezing into a useless mass if you happen to paddle in below freezing conditions.

When you are using twisted polypropylene rope you must be very careful when tying knots. This type of rope has very strong memory characteristics, and any knots you tie tend to undo themselves, and so must be carefully monitored to ensure they remain secure. Free ends should be taped and melted, or crown spliced. If the rope needs to have permanent loops such as in throwbags, the loops should spliced into the rope.

Whenever possible, polypropylene rope should have loops spliced instead of tying knots.

Polypropylene also comes in a braided or woven design which tends to be softer, more flexible, and holds knots more securely. This type of rope is commonly used for water-skiing.

However, both of these types of pure polypropylene rope have some specific disadvantages for paddlers. The main disadvantage is their low strength. There is no comparison between the load capacity and durability of polypropylene and that of nylon, dacron or other synthetic fibre ropes. This lack of strength excludes the use of polypropylene for end loops, anchor ropes, pulling ropes or any other use that demands strength and durability for function and safety. Also, because polypropylene is a very soft, light, low density type of plastic, it has little abrasion resistance and is easily worn and damaged during rough use. It is also very susceptible to heat damage, and any excessive friction caused by running over other ropes or obstacles can result in breakage.

In spite of these shortcomings, polypropylene rope does have its place as long as you do not expect too much from it, and don't use it for purposes it is not designed to serve.

Other Types of Rope

Nylon, polyester, Kevlar, Spectra, and other modern types of synthetic fibre ropes are much stronger. They tend to be softer, easy on the hands, and hold knots very well. The best kind of rope for rescue, is the type which uses "kernmantle" construction; a braided, woven shell which protects a core of continuous strand material. The shell is smooth, providing easy handling and the continuous strand rope inside is very strong. Kernmantle ropes coil easily and resist kinking and twisting much better than do laid or twisted rope.

However, one of the problems associated with some of these ropes is that they absorb more water than pure polypropylene rope. This makes them heavier and reduces their floating characteristics. Another problem is that kernmantle ropes, especially ones designed for climbing, may undergo considerable stretching during loading, and even more so when they are wet. Knots can become so tight that they are virtually impossible to untie. However, the inherent strength and abrasion resistance makes nylon and polyester kernmantle ropes suitable for use in most rescue situations.

Nylon fibre ropes are more expensive than polypropylene rope. The most inexpensive nylon rope is the white, marine nylon rope sold in yachting supply centres and many hardware stores.

White marine nylon rope is quite strong (1500 kg for 9.5 mm) and is a good choice for most water rescue purposes. 9.5 mm white kernmantle nylon is about $2.12/m as compared to $0.40/m for polypropylene, with 12.5 mm rope being $3.57/m and $0.65/m respectively.

The more highly engineered kernmantle ropes, such as those designed for rock climbing and mountaineering, have similar properties, but are more expensive, about $3.00/m. Climbing ropes are meant to keep you from being cut in half when you fall and are therefore very stretchy by design. This elasticity is amplified once the rope gets wet. However, some climbing ropes are constructed using materials and methods which make them "dry", greatly reducing their tendency to absorb water.

In an attempt to bring together the advantages of polypropylene and nylon ropes, manufacturers have produced many types of rope that are a mixture of both materials. These ropes attempt to provide the lightness and water resistance of polypropylene, along with the strength and durability of nylon. Some of the better ropes of this type use a completely synthetic woven outer shell, and a core of polypropylene; a very strong and quite water resistant combination. Unfortunately it is often difficult to find a source for this kind of rope, and a salesman who is knowledgeable enough to be able to tell you exactly what the rope is composed of and what its characteristics are.

No rope containing a high proportion of polypropylene should ever be considered dependable enough to function as a life support line in any kind of vertical or near vertical pull or lower.

The very best rescue rope is a specially designed, dry, static rescue line. These ropes are identical in appearance to a normal, dry climbing rope, except that they are designed not to stretch under load. For anchor lines, river crossing, pulling broached canoes, or as safety lines, these ropes are by far the best. However, although these ropes may be a necessary item for the professional rescuer, they are quite expensive (~$3.30/m) and hard to justify for the recreational paddler.

Which type of rope you choose to use in and around your canoe is a matter of personal preference. However, any group of canoeists, especially river canoeists, should carry at least one 50-metre rescue rope which must be suitable for any rescue that you might be faced with, and which should be readily available at all times.

How to Carry a Rescue Rope

How to carry a rescue rope in your canoe can pose a bit of a problem. To be readily available, the rope should not be carried inside a pack which requires buckles or straps to be unfastened before you have access to the rope. However, carrying a regular coil of rope loose in your canoe can also cause problems. Loose in your canoe the rope will slide around in the bottom getting wet, picking up dirt, and getting stepped on. It will also tend to become tangled even when it is coiled, and will therefore never be ready to be instantly thrown or rapidly uncoiled.

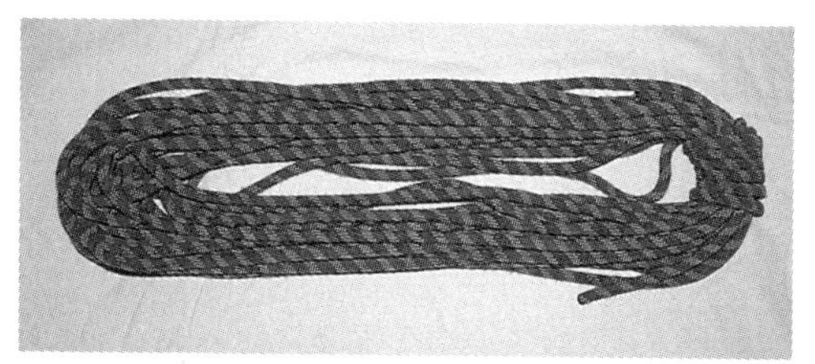

An unprotected coil of rope can become tangled and be difficult to uncoil in an emergency.

The best way to carry a rescue rope is in an individual stuff sack all of its own. This should be a bag made of durable material which is big enough to comfortably hold the entire rope. The rope is stuffed, not coiled, into the bag. When the rope is required, the free end of the rope at the top of the bag is pulled, and the rope can be drawn out smoothly and quickly regardless of how long it has been stored. This method of storage allows you pull out only that amount of rope you need at any particular time.

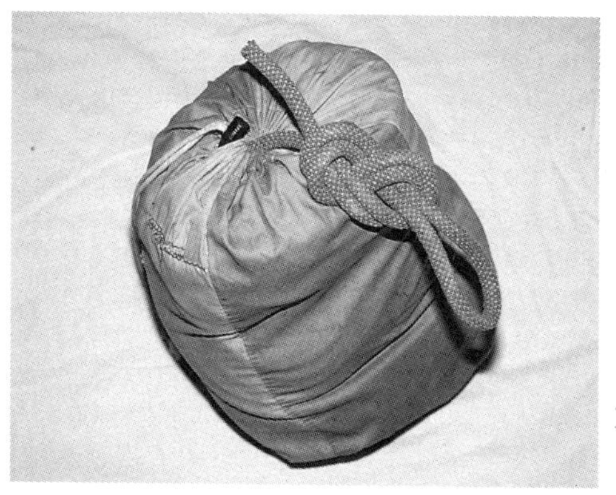

Kept stored in a bag, the rope is quickly available at all times.

Who Should Carry the Rescue Rope

When paddling a river, the rescue rope is usually carried in the last, or most upstream canoe where it will always be approaching an accident scene. It should never be out of reach in a downstream canoe.

Make your Canoe Easier to Rescue

It is important to equip your canoe to make it easier for you to be rescued in an emergency.

Painters

Successful canoe rescues often depend on having some way to grab onto, tow, attach or tie onto the end of the canoe.

I was reminded of this when I once watched a paddler trying to rescue a canoe in a long, continuous, grade two rapid. He was paddling solo, and was attempting to retrieve an abandoned, free floating canoe. The problem was that the capsized canoe had nothing at the ends for the rescuer to grab onto. I watched him grasping and struggling in vain to acquire a hold on the slippery end of the canoe. This process continued as the frustrated rescuer floated past me and finally disappeared around a corner a few hundred metres downstream.

The time honoured method of preventing this problem is to have a painter or line attached to each end of the canoe. If you use a painter make sure it is clear of knots, with no loops, handles or floats which could jam or catch on obstacles in the water.

Painters are often kept loosely coiled in the ends of the canoe. This keeps them readily available to be tossed to a victim, to grab onto if you capsize, or to be used for towing another canoe. However, when you capsize there are two loose ropes floating in the water with you having the potential to cause entanglement, or to become caught up in obstacles.

End Loops

River paddlers often forego the use of painters and favour end loops instead. End loops are 15 cm diameter loops of large diameter rope (11 mm) fixed to the very ends of the canoe. Because end loops must be very strong, they should pass through holes in the hull itself rather than through flimsy deck plates, or small screw-on brackets. End loops are positioned so that the loop hangs just at the water surface. This puts them in easy position for a swimmer to grab onto. It is much easier for a swimmer to maintain a grip on a loop than on a smooth line. Both end loops and painters have their limitations, but I have found that by incorporating both methods, I have a system which provides the greatest versatility in an emergency. I start with a short painter, about 4 m long. One end of the painter is fixed to the end of the canoe by tying it directly to an ordinary end loop. The rest of the painter is coiled and stuffed under a piece of bungie cord mounted on the deck of the canoe. Using this system, the loop is available for the swimmers or rescuers to grab onto, without dislodging the painter. If the painter is required, a quick pull will free it for instant use. The bungie ensures that the painter stays in place even when the canoe is upside down. Whatever system you choose for your canoe, be sure that you understand its limitations.

Strong ends loops are essential for handling canoes.

A deck mounted bungie cord holds a painter firmly in place.

Extra Flotation

River paddlers often put extra flotation in their canoes. This can be anything from an inner tube to large airbags or foam blocks which entirely fill the volume of the canoe. Extra flotation can greatly reduce the chance of swamping and/or capsizing. If you do capsize, the canoe will contain much less water and be less likely to sustain damage, and be less dangerous for the paddler. It will also be lighter and therefore easier to rescue. The drawbacks to this type of flotation are that it may limit the amount of gear that you can carry, and it may also limit your ability to move about in your canoe during a rescue. It may also limit your ability to get a victim into your canoe if the need should arise.

Extra flotation can greatly reduce the chances of swamping, but it must be securely tied in with straps or rope.

Rescue Equipment

Throwbags

A throwbag is a device which allows just about anyone to throw a rope accurately and quickly with a minimum of practice. There is nothing new about throwbags; they have been around since at least WW II, when the navy used them. A throwbag consists of a small nylon bag, with some sort of closure at the top, containing about 20-25 m of rope stuffed or coiled inside. The rope is ready to use; there is no need for any time- consuming uncoiling or untying before the bag is thrown. Although it is a simple device, there are many subtle details which can make one style of throwbag much more efficient than another. While there are many types of commercially made throwbags available, I have never found a commercial throwbag that has all the different characteristics which I require, so I have developed my own design. Throwbags are easy to make, and making your own will allow you to produce a custom product which specifically meets your needs.

For the bag, I use coated nylon packcloth which is strong, reasonably robust and abrasion resistant, as well as being soft and flex-

A homemade throwbag is easy to make, and will fit your own special needs.

A variety of commercial and homemade throwbags.

ible. A problem with bags made of heavier material such as cordura or canvas, is that they tend to "bucket" when they are in the water. Such a bag holds it's shape and acts like a "bucket" on the end of the rope, making the bag slower and more difficult to retrieve, especially in river currents. Once my throwbags are in the water, the softer material allows the bag to collapse and turn inside out, minimizing the resistance to the water, and making retrieval much easier. Some people also use nylon mesh for their bag material. However, I have found that mesh, while providing very little water resistance, has the tendency to always get caught whenever the bag is pulled through branches or other debris. I use bright colours for throwbags. Using a contrasting colour such as red and yellow between the handle and the bag helps the victim to see what to grab onto.

The size of the bag will depend on how much rope you plan to carry, and the diameter of the rope. The bag must be big enough to comfortably contain all the rope. A bag that is jammed tight when all the rope is inside is slower and more difficult to repack. My bags are 30 cm long and about 18 cm in diameter. As a handle, I use a piece of 2.5 cm flat nylon webbing, sewn lengthwise around the bag, with a 10 cm semicircle of webbing at each end. This handle is very useful, not only allowing easy throwing, but slipped over the forearm it supports the bag when repacking, and also provides an easy way of attaching it to your canoe.

A 5 cm strip of velcro at the top of the bag provides secure closure. Most of the other bags I have seen use a pull cord and spring clip to close the bag. This type of closure can be slower to open, especially if the strings become tangled or frozen while they are banging around in the bottom of your canoe.

The next choice is what kind of rope to use. I use 9.5 mm yellow twisted polypropylene for my throwbags. There are number of reason for this choice. First of all it is inexpensive and readily available in most stores. Throwbag ropes can take a good deal of abuse. If you use your throwbag often, up to half a dozen times a day like I sometimes do, the constant dragging over rocks and debris will quickly wear the rope out. When it wears out, I simply replace the rope. Twisted polypropylene is also stiff enough to allow rapid recoiling and stuffing back into the bag, quickly making it ready for re-use.

I use 25 m of rope in the throwbags. One end of the rope goes through a 3 cm hole in the bottom of the throwbag and is spliced around the webbing loop below the bag. Because the handle of the throwbag is directly attached to the rope, it can be used as a handle by the victim without ripping the bag. Inside the bag, the rope passes through a 15 cm diameter disc of 12 mm plywood, which gives shape to the bag and provides some extra flotation. The plywood can also provide a firm handle at the end of the rope. High density foam such as ensolite or camp mat foam can be used instead of plywood. It is softer, therefore to provide firm support for the bag, and to be of use as a handhold, a thick piece of foam is required which decreases the amount of space inside the bag. The other end of the rope has a fist sized loop spliced into it, with a piece of plastic tubing around the rope to make it more comfortable to hold on to.

To pack the bag, pass the webbing loop of the bag handle over your forearm. You can then use both hands to rapidly coil the rope into a handful of fist sized coils. Once you have a handful, stuff them into the bag, and continue the process until all the rope is packed. The rope handle is left half

To repack the throwbag, the rope is coiled into small bundles, and stuffed into the bag.

protruding from the bag, with the velcro closure fastened inside the rope loop. This keeps the bag closed, but also keeps the rope handle immediately and quickly accessible. The bag is now ready for use .

Although I use twisted polypropylene, you can use any kind of rope for your throwbag. If your throwbag is for your own personal use, and won't be used very often, you may want to use a fancier rope. If you use a softer rope, such as a 12 mm mixture of woven nylon and polyprop, you will have to pack it a different way. Soft rope cannot be coiled in small coils quickly enough and then stuffed into the bag. However, the rope can be "run" into the throwbag quite quickly. The way to do this is to again put the throwbag over the forearm and then hang the loose rope over your shoulder. Grasp and pull the rope at your shoulder with one hand, while using the other hand to feed it directly into the throwbag.

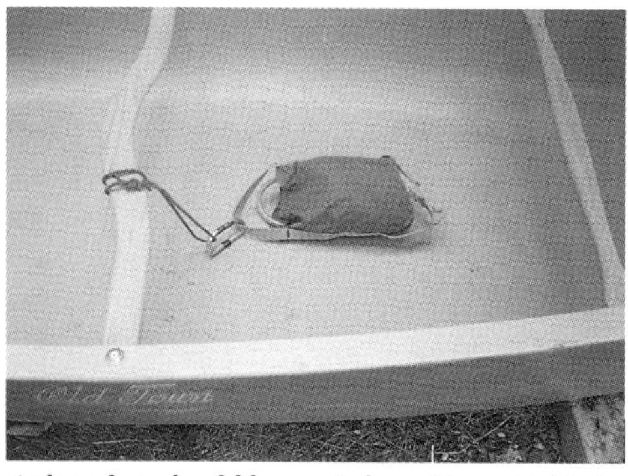

A throwbag should be carried readily available in your canoe at all times.

To be of use, a throwbag must be readily accessible. I carry mine attached to a sling around a thwart by means of a carabiner. They may also be stored in the ends of the canoe, clipped under the deck plates.

Slings

Slings are made from a loop of rope or nylon webbing. Nylon climbing webbing, usually 20-25 mm wide is very strong, with a breaking strength of around 2500 kg. Webbing is often preferred over rope for slings as it takes up less space and can be easily sewn, removing any worry about loose or improper knots. Slings are usually tied to provide a loop about 70-80 cm long. Used in conjunction with carabiners, slings allow rapid and almost foolproof attachment of ropes, and easy and efficient construction of anchor points. They effectively eliminate the time and skill required to tie many knots during a rescue . One or two slings per canoe should be enough for most rescue problems.

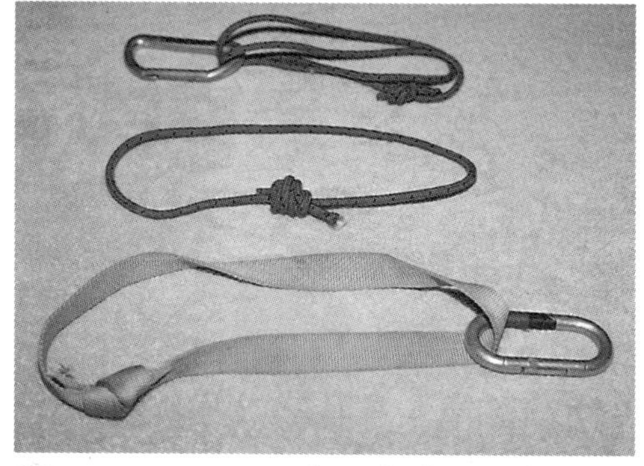

Slings are a very versatile tool. They can be made from rope (top two), or nylon webbing (bottom).

Rescue Pulleys

These small, individual pulleys were originally designed for rock climbing. They twist open so they can be applied anywhere on along the length of a rope. A couple of rescue pulleys can make your rope systems work easier and more efficiently.

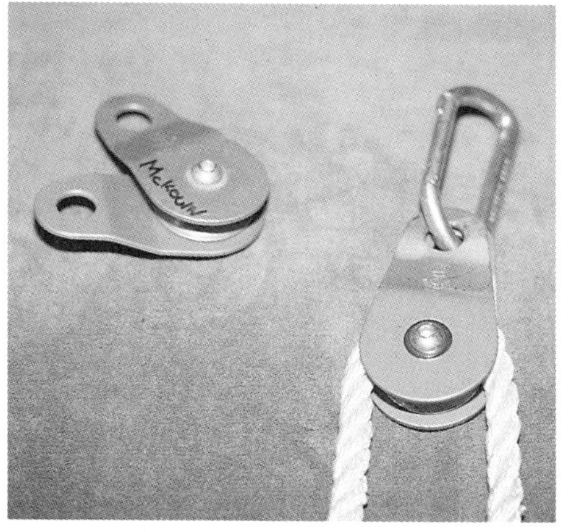

A rescue pulley makes rope systems work more efficiently.

A Rescue Saw

A light weight, collapsible triangular "Sven" saw, or a folding pruning saw, can be a very useful rescue tool. They are inexpensive and easy to carry. Just like a knife, when the time comes that you need a saw, nothing else will do the job. A saw is handy for cutting sweepers, dismantling log jams, or clearing a trail or helipad for an evacuation. It is also great for gathering firewood for that emergency fire. A folding pruning type saw may be more versatile at times than a framed saw as it can cut more easily through boat hulls, or in the dense branches of a log jam. Safer to carry and less easy to cut yourself with than an axe, a saw will cut in confined spaces, and underwater, where an axe might be totally ineffective.

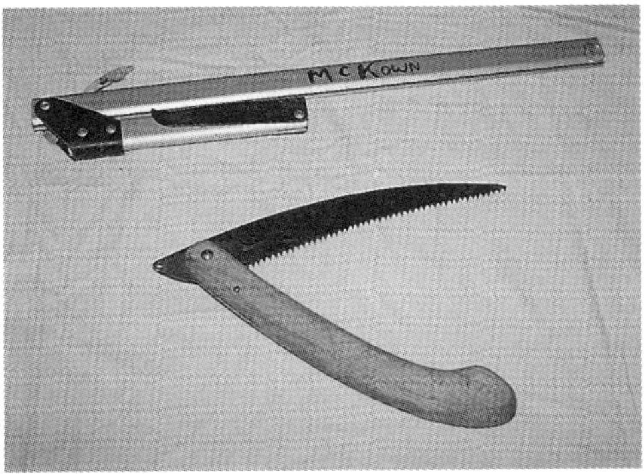

A collapsible "Sven" saw, or a folding pruning saw are useful rescue tools.

Carabiners

Carabiners, fist-sized snap-links made of light alloy with a spring loaded gate, are indispensable in rescue operations. Developed for the climbing community, carabiners are handy for many purposes other than just rescues. One per paddler, or two per canoe will usually provide enough carabiners to conduct most rescues. Carabiners can be purchased with a gate locking device which prevents the gate from opening unexpectedly during use. However, for water rescue I recommend the use of non-locking carabiners, as locking gate carabiners are difficult to apply and remove if you have to reach deep into fast moving water, or if the rescuer is not completely familiar with the device. Carabiners are strong and reliable, with a breaking strength of 1000-2500 kilograms depending on the style you choose. However, because most carabiners are made of aluminum alloy, they will corrode if you spend much time paddling on salt water. Rinse them in fresh water after salt water use, and lubricate the hinge and spring sparingly with a silicone lubricant such as WD40.

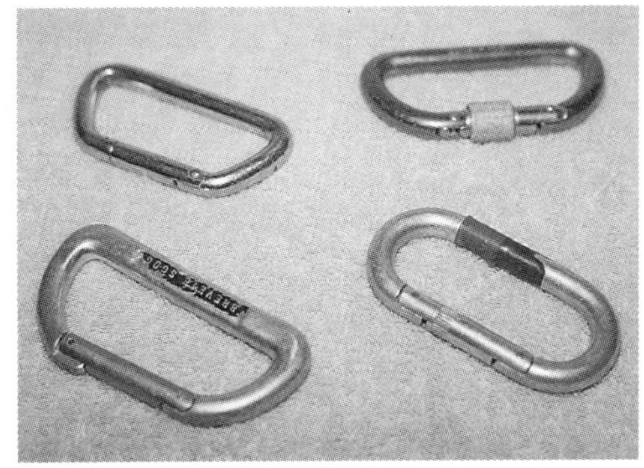

Carabiners are very handy for many canoeing needs, and are indispensable in rescue operations.

First Aid Kit

A first aid kit is an important item for any canoe trip. The group leader must ensure that the first aid kit is up to date, and is well stocked with sufficient supplies for the size of the group. It is also the trip leader's responsibility to see that the pack containing the first aid kit is clearly marked and that all members of the group know exactly where it is being carried. All the members of the group should know who has the most medical training and the most first aid experience. See page 122 for a list of suggested contents of a first aid kit, and the chapter on first aid starting on page 113.

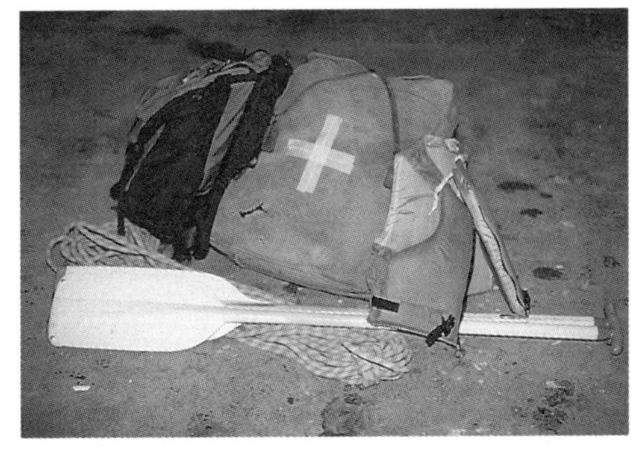

The pack which contains the first aid kit should be clearly marked.

Pacific Rim
National Park
Rivers
the Yukon
Canada
RESOURCE MANAGEMENT
Mackenzie
Forest District
Recreation Map
Saskatchewan
CANOE
TRIPS
number 40
Canoe Trip
54
Saskatchewan
BOOKLET
3
Reach Reports of
the Athabasca
River System
Travel Alberta
BOOKLET
6
River System
FIRST AID SUPPLIES
WILDWATER
Saskatchewan
CANOE
TRIPS
number 19
Saskatchewan
CANOE
TRIPS
number 38

2

Planning for a Safe Trip

Planning a safe canoe trip depends on your being able to properly assess the difficulty and hazards of the route, and in determining what the potential risks are for your group.

The technical difficulty of a trip, such as the whitewater itself, the remoteness, and the weather conditions, are important considerations. There are many sources of information available to the paddler when assessing the difficulty of a canoe trip.

Sources of Information

Information from Other Paddlers

One of the best sources are other competent paddlers who have paddled the particular section in which you are interested. They can give you their opinions of the difficulty and dangers that they encountered. What is particularly important is that they give an opinion from a paddler's perspective, not from the perspective of a rafter or a motorboat fisherman. However, everyone's judgement about river classification and difficulties of a particular route are subjective. If you are asking paddlers whose skill and experience you are familiar with, you will be able to make more accurate decisions than if you are obtaining information from strangers. The stranger's skills and experience are an unknown factor in your decision making equation.

Information From Guidebooks

Guide books and river reports are another good way to gather information about a canoe route. If a guidebook is going to be at all useful, it must always correlate its river descriptions to specific flow rates. However, guidebooks, whether detailed or general, are still providing the subjective judgements of other paddlers about the difficulty of a trip.

Guidebooks must not be considered infallible. Information can be omitted, distances misjudged, and errors can be overlooked. I know of one case where a boater was almost killed and her boat was lost because of an inaccurate description in a guidebook of the take out point above a waterfall. You must therefore keep alert and still be reading the river and assessing the trip ahead rather than relying entirely on the guidebook. Even if it is correct, you could make an error in reading it!

Information from Local Residents

A great deal of information about a canoe route can be gathered from the people who live and work in the area. This includes residents, farmers, forestry workers, fishing camp operators natives, and local guides. Assessing this information must be done with care, as these people may not be paddlers, and their judgements of hazard and difficulty may be completely different from yours. Remember that most of the public have no concept of the capabilities of modern canoes and modern canoeing techniques, so they may paint an overly discouraging picture. On the other hand they may have seen groups of very skilled boaters making a very difficult river look easy. These people may also be able to provide information on more than the water conditions of the route. They may be able to tell you about access points, abandoned road allowances, cabins, camps, the location of radios, and descriptions of the terrain around your intended route.

Information from Local Authorities

The local emergency services may also be able to provide information. Park Wardens, fire departments, police, ambulance services, and forestry service may be able to tell you where on the canoe route there have been problems in the past, and where the significant trouble spots might be. However, since these agencies are likely the ones who are responsible for coming to rescue you in case of an emergency, they may paint an unrealistically discouraging picture of the difficulties, especially as they don't know your capabilities.

Information About Weather and Water Flow

Rivers can change, from season to season, year to year, and even day to day. Your assessment of a river must be based on the particular flow rate and volume that you will be dealing with, which could be very different from the conditions under which your information sources paddled it.

In most areas of North America you should be able to get at least some general information about the water levels in the area you plan to travel in. In Canada, each provincial Department of the Environment office should be able to provide current river flow information. In the United States, the state Forest Service office can usually provide similar information. However, knowing the current water level in a river will not mean very much unless you or your paddling advisor is familiar with the river at that particular flow rate.

Before any canoe trip, it is important to make a full assessment of the weather conditions that you could expect to be faced with. Along with the best current weather forecast, you should contact the weather authorities to find out what the average weather conditions have been over the years, and what kind of extremes of conditions have been known to occur. While weather conditions are of major concern, one must not forget that the knowledge of the water temperature is of critical importance for a paddling trip. This is because water temperature has so much bearing on the seriousness of a capsize. The air temperature can be quite pleasant, but the water may be cold enough to incapacitate a swimmer in a very short time. Harsh weather conditions, freezing cold water, and very remote terrain, increase the hazard of any canoe route.

The difficulty of a river can change dramatically with changes in the volume of water.

Maps

This is not a book about how to read maps. However, maps are an often overlooked aspect of safe canoeing, and knowing how to properly use them can provide a great deal of assistance in carrying out a rescue and evacuation. Maps allow you to plan distances, find routes, pick campsites, and locate access, egress, and bail-out points.

For river paddling, topographical maps will allow you to make some estimation of the gradient of the river and thus make some judgement about the difficulty of the trip.

However, care must be taken with the interpretation of the information found on maps. Topographical maps have two major drawbacks for paddlers. One, is that there is no consistency in the indications of rapids on the maps. Sometimes rapids are shown, and sometimes they are not. Rapids are indicated by one or more lines drawn across the rivers. Although some rapids may be named, some indicated by a capital "R", some labelled as falls, there is no way to determine whether a rapid is large or small, long or short, or is an unlabelled waterfall.

The other problem is that maps rarely if ever give true impressions of vertical cliffs. They simply run the contour lines closely together. From looking at the map, it is impossible to determine whether a steep 50-m slope is a vertical cliff, or something a person could scramble up. There is also no way to determine what lies between contour lines. If a map shows two 30-m contour lines quite far apart, it might indicate a gradual slope. However, there could be a 20-m vertical cliff in-between the contours, and you would never know by looking at the map.

Maps should be prepared before your trip so that the pertinent information is written on them, and readily available to anyone

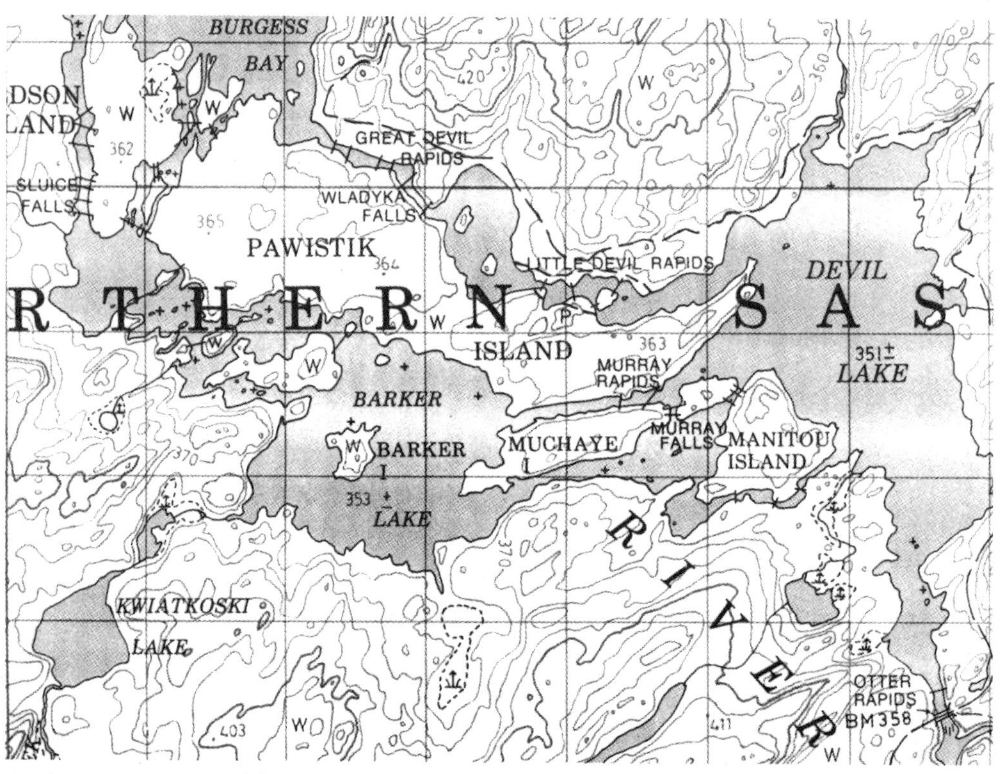

On this topo map some of the rapids are named, some are named as waterfalls, some are only indicated by lines, and there are some rapids in this area which are not shown at all. However, there is no way to tell from the map the extent or difficulty of any of the rapids.

This map is a copy of National Topographic System map sheet number NTS 73 P/10 © 1978. Her Majesty the Queen in Right of Canada with permission of Energy, Mines and Resources Canada.

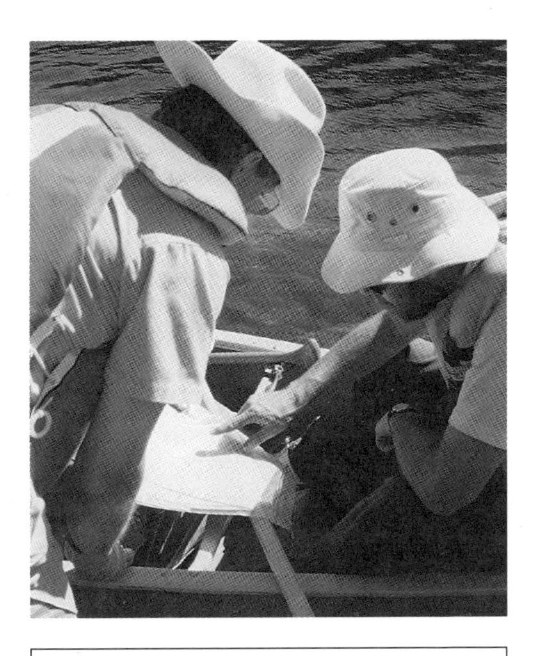

SOURCES OF INFORMATION

Indexes for the topographical maps and aerial photos for Canada, as well as a list of local distributors, are available from:

Canadian Map Office
615 Booth Street
Ottawa, Ontario
K1A OE9
PHONE: 613-952-7000
FAX: 613-957-8861

For the United States, topographical map indexes and the listing of local distributors are available from:

US Geological Survey
1028 General Services Building
19th and F St., NW,
Washington, D.C.,
USA, 20244
PHONE: 202-343-8073

who may be looking at them during a rescue or evacuation. Your main planned route should be indicated on the map, showing your starting and finishing sites. It is also helpful to mark any known access points or possible evacuation routes which may be used in case of emergency. Also highlighted should be the positions of all the radios and telephones for obtaining outside aid. This should include the phone numbers for the local police, park wardens, ambulance, or whatever rescue organizations are available in the area. The location of the nearest hospital and the quickest route to it should also be marked. Make sure that you have enough map coverage for emergency routes as well as your intended route.

A copy of your maps with your intended route should be left with a responsible authority, or at least a good friend, before you leave on your trip. This information should include the number of members in the group, your intended route, and the time you are expected to return.

A group of paddlers should always have at least two full sets of maps, carried in separate canoes.

Most of North America is available in topographical maps of the scale 1:250000. A great deal of North America is available in topographical maps of the scale 1:50000. The 1:50000 scale maps show more detail and are the most suitable for canoeing. Topographical maps are available through outlets in most large centres.

You can also make use of aerial photographs to supplement the topographical maps. Because aerial photos are an actual photograph of the area, they provide exact and more detailed information than do topo maps. They can show you cliffs, rapids, waterfalls, and surface features, much more precisely than can topo maps. Aerial photographs are available for large areas of North America.

Rescue Beacons

Radio rescue beacons can help others to get you out alive if a problem develops in a remote area. However, many paddlers who travel in remote areas seem to have some philosophical bias against taking something that provides any form of radio communications with the outside world. The very reason they go to remote areas is to get away from these technological devices. They almost consider it cheating to carry a rescue beacon; it somehow seems to lessen the feeling of self reliance and independence generated by looking after yourself in the wilderness. A wonderful philosophy, but it doesn't go very far towards explaining to a relative that someone died because although you had the chance to carry a rescue beacon, you chose not to. Whatever your own philosophy, it is for the members of your group to make the decision about whether or not to carry a rescue beacon.

Emergency Position Indicating Radio Beacons (EPIRB's), or Automatic Location Transmitters (ALT's), or Personal Location Beacons (PLB's), are all types of Emergency Locator Transmitters (ELT's). While EPIRBS have been used in other parts of the world, and in the marine and aircraft industry for many years, they are only now becoming popular for personal use in North America. In an attempt to provide some standardization in the development and manufacture of these devices, the Canadian government has, in 1990, made changes in the General Radio Regulations to allow the emergency frequency, 406 MHz, to be used in emergency transmitting beacons, without the need for a license. Currently, there are no EPIRBS manufactured in Canada, and only a few are available in the United States. However, new regulations will allow the manufacturers to build beacons to government standards, and these beacons will soon

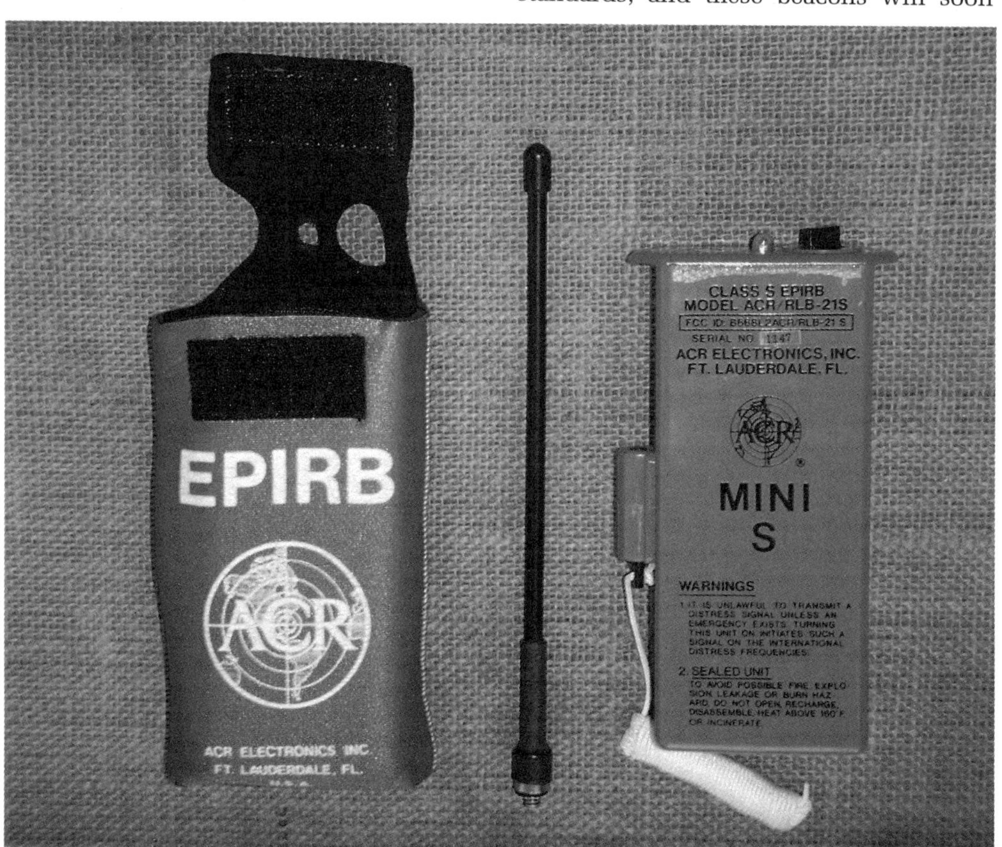

A radio locator beacon, compact and easy to carry, can be a life saving device in a wilderness emergency. They are completely sealed and waterproof making them ideal for canoeing. Photo: Keith Morton

become available in the market place. EPIRBS are the way of the future, and I believe they will soon become a standard piece of equipment for anyone travelling in remote areas.

The EPIRBS that are available today are quite compact and no problem to carry. The most common size is about 18 cm X 8 cm X 5 cm and they weigh about 400 gm. Current prices range from about $450 to $3000, and some equipment outlets will rent them on a daily or weekly basis. These devices, which were originally designed for marine and aircraft use, are completely sealed and waterproof, making them perfect for canoeing.

They are very easy to operate. There is an on/off switch which activates the transmitter as soon as you turn it to the on position. The transmitter should be able to produce a constant signal for at least 48 hours. Once switched on, these devices can be detected by any rescue aircraft that has direction finding receiving equipment. Aircraft so equipped can "home" directly to the location of the transmitting unit. There is also a network of satellites above us, constantly watching our every move, which are designed to pick up the distress signals from EPIRB's and to determine the exact position of the transmitter. This process is a wonderful form of international cooperation. If you are lost in North America, it may be a Russian satellite that will find you. A paddler I know of was in a situation where his EPIRB proved very useful. He had just completed a long wilderness canoe trip across the barren lands of the Northwest Territories. Unfortunately, due to a mix-up in communications, no one knew he needed to be picked up. The abandoned paddler found himself on the desolate shores of the Arctic Ocean, as remote from civilization as only the vast barren lands of the north can make you. After six days, and realizing that no one was on the way to pick him up, he switched on his EPIRB and was rescued in a very short time.

I have personally been involved in two rescues that have been successful as a result of satellite detection of EPIRB transmissions. Without the EPIRB's, none of the people involved in these accidents would have survived.

EPIRB's function as an all or nothing device. Once you turn them on, the wheels are set in motion and somebody will be coming to look for you. Who actually carries out the rescue depends on where you are. The transmissions are usually picked up by military personnel. They will then inform the nearest Coast Guard detachment, or the nearest land forces Search and Rescue Centre. The military may carry out the actual rescue, or notify the local organization which has the responsibility for rescue in your area. This is not the sort of operation that you can easily stop once you have started it. In fact, once you do turn on an EPIRB, you should never turn it off. Doing so confuses the heck out of the entire national rescue system, and may get you into deep trouble. Hopefully, you will never have to use an EPIRB. Still, it can be a nice feeling to know that this option is available when you are involved a major disaster in the middle of nowhere.

GPS Navigation

EPIRB's are a one shot, turn it on, transmitting rescue device.To keep from getting lost, in fact to ensure faultless, effortless navigation, you can use a GPS receiver. These small, hand-held units receive signals from a series of satellites circling the globe. A small display screen will give you your location as either latitude/longitude or as a grid reference using the Universal Transverse Mercator system (UTM). These receivers can be programmed with positions known as "waypoints," which can be stored as a route or used to "go to". You can store the locations of rapids or of desirable campsites and the receiver will help you locate them. As the technology improves and they become more popular their price will go down. The ability to access GPS information through small, completely portable devices represents the future of wilderness navigation.

Physical Hazards

To plan for rescue, and determine the equipment that should be carried, the group leader must find out as much as possible about the physical hazards of the route.

The individual nature of the canoe route, and particularly its own specific physical hazards, will significantly affect your rescue planning. A steep, rocky, technically difficult river will demand a completely different rescue plan, compared to a week long, remote, lake canoeing trip. Unfortunately, it may be difficult to find out what the physical hazards are, so you may need to be prepared for a number of possibilities. The important point is to ensure that all the equipment that is available to your group is suitable for the expected conditions, and that it is in proper working order, before you leave home. I remember a day when one of my friends, Cathy, capsized in a difficult rapid, and there was only one rescuer downstream of her. The rescuer, Steve, jumped out of his canoe, onto the shore to toss his throwbag. Steve was confident in his ability to use a throwbag, and was caught totally by surprise when he swung the bag for a powerful throw, and nothing happened. This was the first time this season that Steve had used this throwbag, and whoever was using the throwbag last had not stored it properly, leaving it stuffed in a tangled, useless mass. Cathy floated by with a forlorn look on her face, and a longer, unpleasant rescue ensued.

How Moving Water Affects Safety

River mishaps are different from lake mishaps in that the river does not stop flowing just because you have an accident. The situation is therefore more dynamic and likely to be more dangerous. Everything, including your rescue, must happen faster, because the situation is continuously changing.

The organization, the planning for rescue, and the establishment of priorities, are exactly the same as for any other emergency situation. However, you are now dealing with moving water, and moving water has an awesome force. The faster the current, the greater the force. Because the amount of force varies directly with the square of the velocity of the water, a very small increase in the velocity produces a large increase in the force of the water.

Most of the time, the power of the river goes unnoticed by canoeists. While you are floating on the river, or even swimming in the water, you rarely appreciate the energy around you. It is only when you try to stop or interrupt the flow of the water that the incredible power of the river becomes immediately apparent. The objective of safe river paddling is to never try to work against the river. The river is indefatigable, it always wins in the end.

Strainers

In the rivers, strainers present one of the greatest dangers to canoeists. Strainers are anything which allows free passage of water, but will catch and hold a solid object such as a canoe or a swimmer. The strainers most often encountered are trees. A strainer is usually first created on the outside of a curve in the bend of a river.

The current undercuts the bank, causing trees to fall into the river.

This is where the speed of the current is strongest, and the river banks are subject to the maximum amount of erosion. As the erosion undercuts the banks, it also undercuts the trees which then fall over until they are hanging straight out over the surface of the water. At this point these trees are called sweepers, since they effortlessly sweep you out of your canoe if you happen to hit one. While they may cause a capsize which could become a problem, sweepers are not usually dangerous in themselves. If you are knocked over by one, you simply float underneath.

I was quite surprised to see this repeated three times one day on a small mountain river. My group was having a lunch break when we saw three, obviously novice canoes, paddling along the side of the river. Just downstream of them were two sweepers, about 20 metres apart. The paddlers in the lead canoe managed to duck down and crash under the first sweeper. However, the second sweeper knocked them over and they were spilled into the cold, glacier water. The interesting aspect of this accident was that the second and third canoe promptly did exactly the same thing. In moments we had 6 swimmers, 3 capsized canoes, and a group of very busy rescuers.

Once the branches of the tree penetrate the surface of the water, the sweeper then becomes a strainer. Now if you are knocked over, or if you are already swimming from a previous capsize, you may not make it through the strainer. You may be caught by the branches, and be held firmly in place by the force of the current. Once this happens, it is extremely difficult or even impossible to get out by yourself. Quick and effective action on the part of your companions may be required in order to save your life.

As undercutting of the bank progresses, and the current continues to press on the branches, the tree may be ripped completely free of the bank. It then floats downstream until it gets grounded on a less deep area. Usually the roots of the stump catch first, and the tree swings parallel to the current, with the stump facing upstream. This is known as a "deadhead", and can also be a dangerous strainer.

Trees hanging above the surface of the water form sweepers.

Once trees penetrate the water surface, they become dangerous strainers.

Deadheads are formed when trees, complete with roots, are torn free from the banks of the river.

Log-jams can create deadly strainers.

Log-jams

Free floating logs and trees will often get hung up at the same obstruction, or even on each other. When this happens a log-jam develops. Log-jams are the worst type of strainers because they can be very large. They can form almost anywhere there is some sort of obstruction in the river for the first log to catch on. They are most dangerous when they form in areas where the current is strong, such as the outside of bends, upstream edges of gravel bars, rocks or bridge abutments, or in narrow, constricted areas. Log-jams can be anything from one or two trees, to huge masses of logs hundreds of feet across, and can become unavoidable river obstacles.

Hydraulics

Next to strainers, re-circulating hydraulics are probably the most dangerous obstacles to be found on rivers. They are also known as holes, souse holes, or keepers. A hydraulic is formed at a location where the water flows over a steep shelf or ledge, like a small waterfall, into a low gradient pool or relatively flat river bottom. The current then boils up to the surface, and flows back upstream towards the face of the drop. This water flow pattern acts as a powerful recirculating system that can be impossible for a paddler to escape from. The amount of danger presented by any individual hydraulic is a function of a number of factors; the height and steepness of the drop, the depth and slope of the river bottom at the base of the drop, and the amount and speed of the water going over the drop. Of particular importance is the uniformity of all these things across the extent of the drop. The most dangerous type of hydraulic is formed by artificially constructed,

Opposite: Steep ledges and drops should be carefully assessed as they may be dangerous, recirculating, hydraulics.

The consistent uniform structure of man made weirs creates inescapable drowning machines.

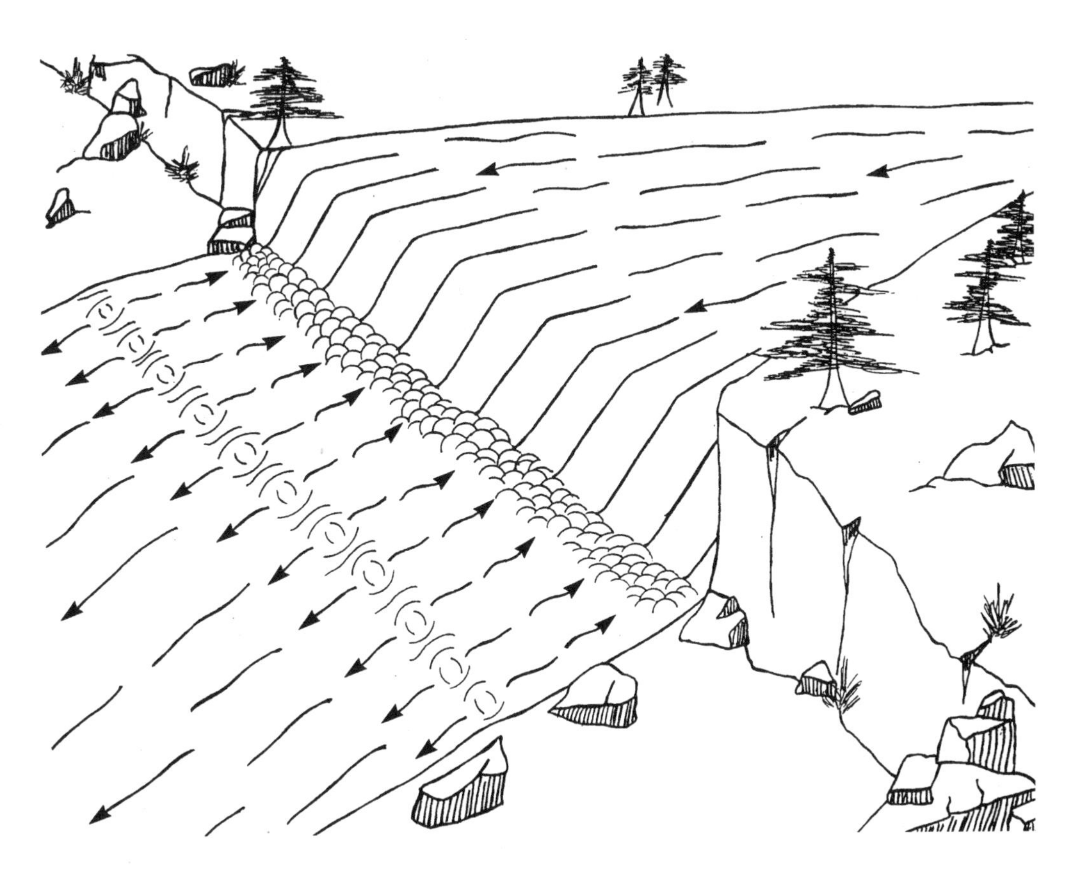

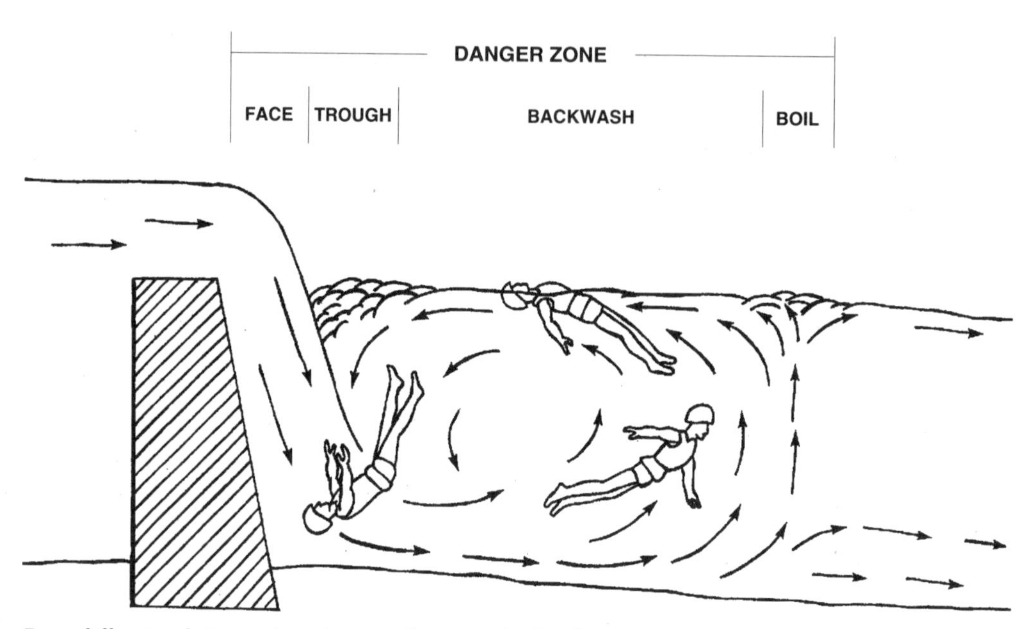

Powerfull recirculating systems in steep drops can be deadly traps for paddlers.

low head dams or weirs. Because of the very steep faces, and particularly the exact uniformity of these constructions, they can be virtually inescapable drowning machines. However, very dangerous hydraulics can also be formed by naturally occurring ledges and waterfalls in a river. The importance of hydraulics is that you must be able to recognize them, and determine what is dangerous and what is not. The ability to read a river and judge what is a dangerous keeper hole, and what is a safe hole, requires experience. A ledge across a river may be very dangerous in some areas, but it might also have chutes and breaks in it which are quite runnable. As a general rule, any feature you encounter where the water drops steeply over a rock, shelf, or ledge, should be suspect and carefully assessed. Dangerous hydraulics should be avoided at all times.

Rocks and Boulders

The other major hazard on rivers for canoeists are rocks and boulders. Because rocks are solid, immovable objects which force the flow of current around them, individual rocks and boulders do not form strainers and do not cause the same problems as trees. If you are in the water and swimming, the current will most often carry you around individual rocks. The major danger that rocks represent is the possibility of being caught between the rock and a canoe full of water. A canoe full of water moving at any kind of speed can have several tons of force. This force is more than enough to cause serious injury or death if you are caught between the canoe and a rock, or other obstruction. Once you are caught, and possibly injured, you can remain pinned, as the current continuously presses on the canoe holding you in place. In addition to the possibility of personal injury, rocks also represent the potential for catching canoes so they become broached and pinned around the rock by the current.

However, a group of rocks can also act as a strainer. Small channels between rocks can allow free flow of water but still be small enough to prevent the passage of canoe or paddler. Rocks can be small strainers as well, catching your foot or ankle while the current prevents you from freeing yourself. If your foot becomes stuck and the water is deeper than your knees, the force of the water can easily push you over. The current can make it impossible for you to pull yourself upright, especially if your ankle was broken in the process of becoming trapped. You end up pinned in the water by the force of the current, and can very rapidly drown. It is recommended that you never attempt to stand up in fast water that is deeper than your knees. When the water is less than knee deep, there should be less chance of being pushed over even if you do get a foot stuck.

Entrapment is also possible in places where rocks and cliffs are eroded away and undercut by the current. Swimmers and canoes can be carried and pushed into undercuts, where they may be firmly pinned by the force of the current. Rock undercuts can be very dangerous as they often occur in sites which provide very little, or very difficult and hazardous access to the victim by the rescuers.

Assessing the potential dangers caused by rocks and trees is not easy. Any river with forested banks has the potential for sweepers and strainers to form. The more bends in the river, and the more obstacles present, the more likely it is to have log-jams and sweepers. Poor logging practices along a river can also provide a great deal of fodder for the formation of log-jams.

An undercut rock on the outside of a bend. Even at low water, as in this picture, a canoe or canoeist could be pinned. In higher water the danger is much more significant because of stronger currents flowing downwards under the undercut and the greater possibility of the canoeist being pinned underwater. Photo: Keith Morton.

Putting the Information Together

Once you have gathered all the information from various sources, and considered the physical hazards and all the other factors, you are in a position to correlate all this information and to make your final assessment of the overall technical difficulty of a canoe trip. You can now determine what skill levels are required in your paddling group.

The individual in the position of group leader or trip leader is responsible for assessing the skill level of the individual paddlers. Anyone whose skills are not at a sufficient level for a particular trip must be informed, and excluded from the group. This is the only safe option for the rest of the members of your group. Taking insufficiently skilled paddlers on a difficult canoe trip only puts the other paddlers at risk. Remember that the rest of the group must put their own safety on the line if the less experienced paddlers get into trouble.

I have seen this problem of paddlers getting into situations over their heads many times. One morning during a whitewater course, I was discussing paddling techniques with my group, on a continuous, very technical, grade 2-3 mountain river. One of the students pointed upstream, as a canoe paddle floated around the corner, down the rapid towards us. This was soon followed by a blanket, and then an object which appeared to be part of a child's car seat. By this time I was out of my canoe, and running upstream along the shore. Around the corner I found a man and his fourteen year old son, crawling up the riverbank. In a couple of minutes, another man came around the corner, dragging a sixteen foot fiberglass canoe. These were completely novice paddlers. They had seen a good looking starting point a few hundred metres upstream, put their canoe in the water and headed off downriver. Luckily, they had swamped and capsized in the first few metres. These paddlers had absolutely no idea of what was downstream of them. They were completely surprised to hear about very technical grade three rapids, steep ledges, and continuous powerful currents. While soaking wet, rubbing his hands together to try and warm them up, the father quite seriously asked me if I thought they could make it down the river. The son showed a little more intelligence. He stood shivering in the cold, repeating again and again, "I'm not getting back into that canoe, I'm not getting back into that canoe...". I managed to talk them all into going home.

Once you have assessed all the technical difficulties and physical hazards of your trip, you will be in a much better position to plan for rescue. You can determine what kind of equipment will best suit your situation, how much equipment may be necessary, and which rescue techniques are going to be most successful under the expected conditions.

Safety Considerations when Paddling Alone

I should say a word here about paddling alone. I personally have nothing against paddling alone. People have successfully travelled thousands of miles in canoes on their own. However, if you choose to canoe by yourself you must first accept full responsibility for your own safety. When you are by yourself and something goes wrong, you are totally on your own. There are things you can do, especially if you're properly equipped and have a good rescue plan, but your options are very limited. If you become hurt during the accident, your ability to carry out a self rescue is extremely limited. If you are alone, you must also consider the fact that even though there may be no one to report the accident to, other people will eventually be looking for you. This means that, sooner or later, other people are going to be possibly putting themselves at risk because of your decision to paddle alone.

Even having just one other person with you vastly increases your chances of survival. For lake travel, two canoes are the recommended minimum number necessary for safety. On a river, three boats are considered essential if safe and efficient rescues are to be carried out.

Group Preparation for Dealing with Emergencies

Knowing the Abilities of Each Member of Your Group

Safety and rescue planning begins with finding out about the people with whom you will be paddling. The more you know about the skills and aptitudes of every individual in your group, the more efficiently you will be able to work as a team in times of emergency. In the middle of a rescue is not the time to find out who can or cannot tie the knots or perform the required skills.

First and foremost, you should determine the paddling skill levels of every member of the group. This is best done by paddling with them to see how proficient they are. You also need to find out what level of skill you can expect them to provide at the scene of an emergency, because as a rescue leader, you must be able to delegate tasks. You should never delegate tasks to individuals who do not have the necessary skills to carry them out. Who is comfortable with rigging ropes and tying knots? Who are the strongest swimmers, and who has the most first aid training and experience? You need to know the answers to these questions before you have to conduct a rescue. When everyone is aware of the abilities of the others, it is much easier during an emergency situation to assign tasks to individuals in ways which best utilize their skills and experience. I always feel more comfortable paddling with people with whom I have canoed many times before because I know their experience and skill levels, and what I can depend on them to do.

On any canoe trip, be it a few hours, a couple of days, or an extended tour, there should be a group leader who is responsible for the organization of the group. However, information about the members of the group should not be held only by that one individual. Although a specific rescue leader should be designated at the beginning of the trip, when an emergency happens, anyone in the group may find himself in the position of rescue leader. Every individual must therefore be as knowledgeable as possible about every other member of the group. As well, each member of the group should be aware of what rescue equipment is available, and who is carrying it. A rescue is always quicker, more efficient, and safer if all members of the group can provide the required assistance in an emergency.

Group organization includes practice, or at the very least discussion, with all members of your group, about what procedures you will follow in the case of any accident. This allows everyone to know what to expect when they capsize or when some other critical incident develops. All members must be aware of what sequence of rescue techniques to expect, what signals will be used, and what resources are available.

Knowledge of the physical condition of the members of the group is of prime importance when planning for emergencies. You should discuss as a group any medical conditions which could become a problem, and make plans to deal with them if necessary. Medical conditions which should be known to the group include asthma, diabetes, epilepsy or heart conditions. They would also include allergies to insect bites or to particular foods. If a person carries medication for an allergy, all members of the group should know where it is kept and how to properly administer it.

Organizing Your Group for Safe Lake Travel

Although it might seem unlikely that you can get into serious trouble while canoeing on a lake, problems can arise very easily. Lakes are usually considered to be a stable, controlled environment for paddling, and canoeists on a lake can easily get lulled into a false sense of security. Then, before they even realize it, the wind comes up, the rain starts, and now they can't see the rest of the canoes. The shore is further away than they thought, and it's directly into the wind, or is no good for landing anyway. Two canoes are considered the minimum number required for safe lake canoeing. This allows for one canoe to be available to go for help, and also provides more rescue options during an emergency. Canoes are classed as in-shore craft and are not designed to cross large bodies of open water. If a capsize does occur on a lake, hopefully the canoe is close to shore. If your route demands the crossing of a large stretch of open water, then you should assess the conditions very carefully, and only cross when the conditions are as suitable and stable as possible. This is usually in the early morning or late evening when the winds are at their most calm.

During a canoe trip, weather conditions are always a prime concern for paddlers. Although no one can predict exactly what the weather will be in the future, canoeists must constantly make judgements about coming changes in weather patterns. In many areas, the weather can deteriorate amazingly quickly. If paddlers aren't paying close attention, they may rapidly find themselves in the midst of driving rain and powerful winds. The more accurate your are in your weather forecasting, the more likely you are to stay out of trouble. Paddlers should always be alert for clues, such as, the appearance of different types of cloud formations, a rapid drop or rise in temperature, or a change in the direction of the prevailing winds. All of these indicators can herald a coming change in the existing weather pattern. For paddlers trying to plan a safe day of canoeing, there is a simple rule of thumb. If there are any clues which have you wondering if the weather is going to deteriorate, it probably is, and you should plan accordingly.

Weather can deteriorate rapidly, and create hazardous conditions for paddlers very quickly.

To maintain safety when you are on the water, keep your group properly organized, and together. There should be a designated lead canoe and a designated tail canoe in the group, and everyone should be aware of the position of all the other canoes at all times. The general rule is that each canoe is responsible for the safety and well being of the canoe behind them. As long as everyone pays attention, this procedure should ensure that no canoe gets into trouble unnoticed, or gets left behind. Making sure that everyone **does** pay attention can be the problem. If your safety is going to depend on your fellow paddlers, you must be familiar with their attitudes and abilities before you go on a trip with them.

This became apparent to me during a week long canoe trip with a group of paddlers who did not know each other very well. Some of the group was interested in paddling continuously, to cover as much distance as possible. The rest of the paddlers wanted to do some photography and fishing along the way. This group spent a great deal of the trip with a number of canoes completely separated and out of touch with the others. Luckily, the weather was fine and no problems developed.

In the event that the group does somehow get separated, each paddler should know their exact position at all times, and be familiar with the planned route for the day. There should be pre-planned times and points for group rendezvous so that the trip leader can ensure that no problems are developing.

Looking back upstream. Paddlers are always responsible for the canoeists behind, or upstream of them.

Organizing Your Group for Safe River Travel

On a river, the designated tail boat of the group is responsible for ensuring that all boats stay downstream of him, and that the group does not get overly spread out.

Between the lead boat and the tail boat it is usually a free for all, with positions changing continuously. As long as no one passes the lead canoe or gets upstream of the tail canoe, the group should not get separated. However, at any given moment each paddler is still responsible for the canoe upstream of him, and must pay close attention to the condition of other paddlers. The importance of this was brought home to me during an accident about twenty years ago. I was canoeing solo with a group of paddlers whom I didn't know particularly well. My two friends who had originally planned to be part of the group had a change of plans and were unable to participate. We were paddling a beautiful, wilderness river, with picturesque canyons, and some excellent rapids and rock gardens. My problems began after about an hour of paddling, when I capsized while running a four foot ledge in a narrow canyon. The current was powerful here and the river was deep and fast. I only managed a small gasp of air before I was hammered under by the river. It seemed like an eternity that I was underwater. It must have been a while, because to this day I can still remember the water getting blacker and blacker as I was swirled to the bottom of the canyon. I can still remember thinking that I would not have enough air to get back to the surface. I eventually did come up, quite a distance downstream, and just managed to get to shore. I was very shaken up, weak and nauseated. Someone had rescued my canoe and brought it to shore. I crawled back into the canoe in a bit of a daze, and prepared to continue. The rest of the paddlers assumed I was fine and off we went. But I wasn't fine. I couldn't control the canoe very well, and still felt quite weak and light headed. None of my companions realized that I was in no condition to paddle. I dropped further and further behind. In one of the large, powerful rock gardens I finally lost it completely and crashed over a huge boulder. At this point, the rest of the group was already out of sight down the river. I had a long, nasty swim before finally dragging myself ashore. Nothing was broken, but I was thoroughly beat up. My canoe was stuck on a rock

Scouting rapids and always being aware of what is downstream, are important aspects of river safety.

out in the river, my paddle was gone. Things were looking pretty grim, but, after a little rest, I did manage to get my canoe to shore. There were two large holes, luckily above the water line, a broken seat, and numerous cracks. I searched around on the shore and was able to find a piece of driftwood to use as a paddle. Somehow, and its probably just as well that I can't exactly remember, I managed to survive the next five kilometres of grade three rapids to reach the take out point. Surprisingly enough, the rest of the group was beginning to wonder where I had gotten to! It was a hard lesson to learn, but this episode certainly created a memorable day of paddling for me.

In small groups the lead boat and tail boat often changes as everyone is eddy hopping, and maneuvering on the river. This is fine, but only in small groups when everyone can always be aware of the positions of all of the other boaters.

Group organization and safety means maintaining control of the group, especially at difficult sections and rapids. On an unknown river, the general rule is to never paddle past your last safe stopping eddy. Paddlers must scout the river until they find an eddy in which they are certain that all the boats in the group will be able to stop safely and easily, and where they will be able to complete any necessary rescues resulting from incidents upstream of this point. If paddlers cannot see the next clear stopping eddy, then they must get out of their canoes and keep on scouting .

If there is a significant chance of a capsize, it is good practice for the group to set up for rescue before running the rapid. This may mean that one or two canoes are portaged to the stopping eddy, to act as safety boats, and one or two rescuers are positioned at likely points along the rapid with throw ropes. In any difficult sections, the canoes run the rapid one boat at a time so that only one rescue should be required at any given moment. Signals must be arranged so that the next boat in the group does not begin the run until the previous boat is clear.

Even on rivers that you are familiar with, continually look ahead for your next stopping eddy, and scout rapids which are not clearly visible from the canoe for their entire length. Rivers can change very quickly. Sweepers and strainers can be created overnight, turning a previously harmless section of river into a deadly trap.

Communications and Signalling for Maintaining Group Safety

On a river as well as on a lake all paddlers, not just the group leader, are responsible for safety. The group leader may only be able to see one or two canoes at a time, so the general rule is that every canoe is responsible for the canoe behind, or upstream, of them. As a paddler, you are responsible for knowing if the canoe behind you is in trouble, wants to stop, or is getting too far behind. Not only are you responsible for continuously knowing this information, but also for passing it on to the boat in front of you, so that it quickly reaches the lead canoe of the group. Too many times I've seen accidents happen, especially on rivers, and the first the lead boat learns about it is when a capsized canoe floats by. To paddle safely, it is important to be able to pass information quickly among the group. Clear communications are the key to preventing route finding errors, to warn of rapids, and to carry out successful rescues.

Everyone you are paddling with should be familiar with the system of signals that you plan to use. Planning and consistency are important in the use of signals, or the signals themselves can be more of a hazard than a help. One of my friends found this out the hard way. We were paddling a large Canadian Shield river, with high volume, pool and drop rapids. There were quite a mixture of paddlers from beginner to expert, and a variety of open canoes, closed canoes, and kayaks. Because a couple of paddlers in the group had run this section before, we had made no definite plans about river signals and, for the most part, had no need to scout the rapids. At one particularly interesting rapid, the river dropped steeply through a chute, and around a large shelf of rock. The current then split into two channels, one clear channel, and one where the current piled into an enormous boulder. Three of us had just finished running the drop when the mistake was made. Glen was the last paddler, a relative beginner, who had just finished his run and was quite excited. He had not known about the second channel, and when he saw it, he got even more excited, and decided that he must warn the rest of the paddlers about this hazard. It was too noisy for the remaining paddlers up above to hear Glen's shouts over the sound of the rapid, although they could see him quite clearly. Instead, Glen used his paddle blade, and vigorously pointed to the right, trying to indicate the hazard present in that route. My friend Tom was next in line to run the drop. Tom was an experienced paddler, and in the system of signalling that he was familiar with, the canoeist always uses the most easily seen part of the paddle, the blade, to indicate the correct route. Tom made his run down the right channel. Coming through the chute, he maneuvered into the right channel, and only then did he realize the extent of his error in judgement. Tom was completely helpless. He and his canoe were flushed down the channel, and slammed into the giant boulder. However, Tom was a quick thinker, and just as his canoe crashed into the immovable granite, he made a less than graceful bail out to the side, and was washed around the boulder into the calm water below. Tom's canoe was hammered against the boulder, and disintegrated almost instantly under the driving impact of the powerful current. Tom survived the incident with no ill effects, but his canoe was totally destroyed. Tom was not a happy man, and he became a passenger in Glen's canoe for the rest of the trip.

Signals can be a big help in increasing the safety of a canoe trip, but like all procedures, they must be developed, planned, and discussed before the trip begins.

The key to successful communications by signal is to keep the system as simple as possible. People are not going to be able to remember a lot of different signals, especially in a time of stress, and there may not be time for many different signals.

I use two different systems of signals. One for audio, one for visual. Audio signals, using whistles, work well, depending on the ambient noise level. On a busy river this may be a very short distance. On a lake it may be up to a kilometre. Unfortunately, there is no universally accepted set of signals. The system I have developed seems logical and has worked for me for many years.

Audio Signals

One blast to get attention. This is usually in preparation for passing on other information, either by audio or visual signals.

Two blasts on a whistle means a paddler wants to stop. This is a non-emergency. It may be used by the lead boat to stop the group and scout rapids, or by another paddler that needs to stop and empty his boat or his bladder. When this signal is heard, the information is passed up to the lead canoe and the entire group is brought to a halt.

Three blasts on the whistle means there is a problem. A boat has capsized, or a paddler is in trouble. This information must also be passed up to the lead canoe so that the group can be stopped, and rescue procedures initiated.

This is about the limit of information that you can hope to deliver consistently with audio signals. Because of the limitations of audio signals due to distance and ambient noise, it is also useful to have a visual signalling system as well.

Visual Signals

A canoe paddle makes an excellent signalling device because all paddlers have one in their hands most of the time. Again I keep my system as simple and clear as possible. Basically, signals indicate that the paddlers should follow the blade of the signalling paddle. If the signaller holds the paddle straight up, with blade at the top, it indicates "follow me" or "this is the proper route".

If the signaller holds the paddle above his head with the blade facing to the left, it means the route is to the left. If he holds it up with the blade pointing to the right, then the proper route is to the right. If he holds the paddle straight up with the blade at the top and waves it continuously back and forth, this is the stop signal. It may mean a problem or emergency, or it may be used to mean that someone just has to stop for some reason.

These are about the only signals that are clearly distinguishable from any distance on a lake or river. However, you must always keep in mind that visual signals will only work if the canoeists are looking in the right direction.

These signals should provide enough control to at least get your group stopped if a problem arises. If more precise signals are necessary during an actual rescue or recovery, then they can be set up at the time by the rescue leader.

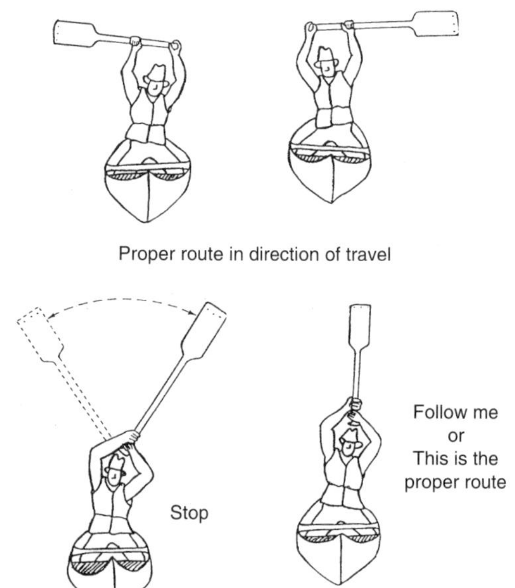

Loading Canoes and Storing Gear to Provide the Most Rescue Options

While it's an obvious precaution in rivers, lake paddlers often see little need to tie their packs to the canoe. However, it is often quite helpful to have your packs secured to the canoe, and it is most advantageous if all members of the group secure their gear with the same system. The primary reason for tying the gear to the canoe is to keep the gear and the canoe together when you capsize. While it may be easy to keep track of things in calm water, rough weather and poor visibility could make losing track of free floating packs a very real possibility. I have found that tying the packs directly to the thwarts of the canoe greatly reduces the options available to you during a rescue. It prohibits the use of the throwover method, and the T-rescue, two mainstays of canoe rescue techniques. It also makes it very difficult to turn a canoe over and empty it without untying and removing the packs. This can be a problem if you need to empty the canoe often or if you find yourself stuck in a shallow mid-river eddy, or standing knee deep in moving water, hanging onto a swamped canoe. There is nothing more frustrating for me than paddling up to a swamped canoe, prepared to quickly help someone empty it, only to find a totally unmanageable situation because of heavy packs tied directly to the thwarts. To solve this problem I have found it best to tie the packs to the canoe by means of a 3-metre long piece of rope. The exact length is not important as long as the final distance between the packs and the tie in point on the midthwart is at least one half the length of the canoe. The packs are stowed in the canoe with the rope clear, to ensure that during a capsize, the packs will float completely free of the canoe. This allows the canoe to then be recovered by whichever means is appro–priate. It can be thrown over, emptied, or T-rescued simply and quickly, and the packs can them be returned to the canoe.

Good group organization for handling emergencies also includes the appropriate distribution of resources among the group. Rescue equipment and first aid supplies should not all be carried in the same canoe. Similarly, regular supplies, such as food, tents, sleeping bags, and cooking equipment should also be distributed among all the paddlers. Each canoe should be as much of a self sufficient unit as possible. This ensures that the loss of one canoe will not put the entire group at risk.

However, it is recommended that you carry the main rescue tools, such as the rescue rope and first aid kit, in the last canoe of the group so that equipment will always be approaching an accident scene, not travelling away from it. On a river this would be the tail boat, or most upstream canoe in your group.

3

The Rescue Plan

Safe paddling must be an ongoing procedure. It is the reflection of a psychological attitude, and should be continuously practised. This doesn't mean that to paddle safely you can't have any fun. It just means that all paddlers must maintain a constant awareness of their situation and that of others, so that when someone's judgement goes amiss, a critical incident is not allowed to deteriorate into a disaster.

It is impossible to over emphasize the importance of pre-trip rescue planning on your ability to canoe safely, and particularly, to handle rescue situations when they arise. Because many of the factors which lead to the development of critical incidents and emergency situations are predictable, you can plan to avoid them or to deal with them more effectively.

Prepare Yourself Psychologically

Proper preparation for emergencies is more than the physical accumulation and control of resources. It also involves ensuring that you are psychologically and emotionally prepared to deal with a critical situation. As anyone who has been involved in competitive sporting activities can tell you, winning has a great deal to do with the competitor's state of mind. If you can't win the psychological battle, you will surely lose the physical one. When a canoeing accident happens, there are many factors involved that will influence the state of mind of the rescuer. The amount of pre-planning and preparation the rescuer has made will directly affect his mental and emotional stability when an emergency arises.

When an accident happens, a leader who has not planned his travelling organization can become rapidly frustrated because the other members of the group are likely to be in a poor position to carry out the rescue. If the rescuer does not have the equipment and physical resources available to do the job, he feels helpless in the face of the emergency. If the rescuer has no repertoire of skills and training, he is powerless to develop a rescue plan. This leads to feelings of fear, tension, and uncertainty in his ability to deal effectively with the emergency. Add to this the guilt which develops from realizing that he was unprepared, and you have a rescuer who is half defeated before he even begins. When directing an emergency situation, a hesitant and insecure rescue leader rapidly spreads this attitude of fear, frustration, and helplessness among the other rescuers.

However, a properly prepared paddler is, psychologically, already well on the way to being able to conduct a successful rescue. When you are following an organized plan in your travel procedures, you know that everyone will be aware of the situation of all the others in the group, and be in the best position possible to respond in case of an emergency. This reduces assessment time and limits frustration. The availability of equipment and resources diminishes fear and hesitation. A little bit of practice and training provides knowledge of options, and alternatives in developing an appropriate rescue plan. This rescue leader is confident, and knows that he will be able to do the best job he can. A confident, assured rescue leader immediately inspires confidence in the rest of the group. He reduces tension and frustration throughout the group, increases hope, and is much more likely to lead a successful rescue.

The Role of the Rescue Leader

Carrying out a successful rescue requires you to follow a definite sequence of steps which ensure that all the necessary procedures are completed and that nothing is overlooked. In order to do this as efficiently as possible, someone at the scene of an accident must immediately assume the role of rescue leader. Initially, the rescue leader will be the first rescuer to arrive on the scene. Then, as more people arrive, responsibility should be transferred to the designated rescue leader who was identified at the beginning of the trip, and who will normally be the most experienced member of the group.

The job of a rescue leader is a complex one. As a rescue leader you must direct the rescue, making sure that all necessary tasks are carried out, keep the rescuers out of trouble, and at the same time keep the rescuers motivated and confident of a successful outcome.

In order to direct a rescue efficiently, the rescue leader must not be distracted, and therefore should not become actively involved in the rescue if at all possible. There may be many individual tasks which must be completed in order to carry out a successful rescue, and the rescue leader must delegate all of these tasks to those individuals most able to carry them out effectively. The leader must also maintain an overview of the entire operation to ensure that all aspects of the rescue are being attended to, while at the same time assessing the success of the rescue, and be preparing a secondary plan in case the first one fails.

As rescue leader you have the responsibility for the entire rescue. To function in this position you must have the wholehearted support and cooperation of all the other participants. The rescuers must function together as a team, because during an emergency, seconds count, and efficiency is of paramount importance. Consequently, in an emergency, orders must be given directly and be obeyed instantly; emergencies and rescue scenes cannot be directed by a committee. You should be prepared to solicit and accept suggestions and advice, but your decisions are final and must be carried out without question. You must also be prepared to hand over the rescue leader's position if another individual with more training and experience arrives on the scene and is willing to accept the responsibility.

Determining Priorities in an Emergency

When you deal with an emergency in canoeing, you are dealing with incidents which have the potential to cause injury or even develop into a life threatening situation. Because you are faced with the potential of very serious consequences, you must develop priorities which allow you to best minimize those consequences, which may include the possibility of further injury or death.

In this respect, canoe rescue is no different from any other kind of emergency situation, and you can apply standard rescue priorities to canoeing incidents.

The basic priority for handling an emergency, whether it is a medical problem, a car accident, a mountain rescue, or a canoe rescue, is always the same. This is, that whatever action you take, you should not make the situation any worse, or cause any further injury to the victim.

When an accident does happen it is usually a time of chaos and fear. Feelings run high, and it can be very tempting to jump right in and try to save the victim immediately. However, during an emergency the victim is not the first priority. Your own safety must always be your number one priority. There is no point in getting involved in a dangerous situation with the victim if it is going to put you at risk of injury as well. Remember, your prime objective is to prevent the situation from becoming any worse. If the rescuer gets into trouble, you have just doubled the entire problem and made things twice as difficult for the rest of the group.

Once you have ensured your own safety, you must make certain that the rest of the group is protected so that the problem does not get any worse. For example, if you are paddling down a river and the boat in front of you goes over a waterfall, the first thing you do is paddle to shore to protect yourself. Then you stop the rest of the group and inform them about the waterfall. Only when you are safe, and the rest of the group is protected, can you turn your attention to the victim. The priorities of all rescues are therefore; **Protect yourself, protect the others, then proceed with the rescue.** These basic priorities must be applied throughout the entire rescue.

Determining the Risk/Benefit Ratio of a Rescue

Almost all canoeing emergencies create some degree of risk for the rescuers. You, the rescuer, must make a judgement as to what level of risk is acceptable for a given benefit or result. This is known as the "risk/benefit ratio" of a rescue operation.

To properly perform a rescue demands a constant evaluation of the risk and of the possible benefits, during the entire rescue procedure. For example, it might be acceptable to perform a rescue involving a high degree of personal risk to get to a trapped paddler quickly, and to lift his head above water before he drowns. However, it may be totally unacceptable to perform a rescue with the same level of personal risk to retrieve a broached canoe, or a canoeist who is certainly dead.

The evaluation of the risk/benefit ratio is your responsibility as the rescue leader. It must be constantly on your mind because it changes throughout the course of the rescue. You should be prepared to take the bigger risks at the beginning of the rescue, when the victim is most likely to survive. As time progresses and the chance of survival fades, the potential for receiving benefits diminishes and it may be inappropriate to continue rescue operations which present a significant risk.

Operating in "Rescue Mode"

During the period of potential high benefit, you should operate in what is known as "rescue mode". At this time you are working flat out, as hard as possible, and some personal risk may be acceptable if there is a strong chance of saving the victim. Extreme care must be taken as this is the time when accidents to the rest of your party are likely to happen. The emergency can be made rapidly worse if the rescue leader is not concentrating fully on every aspect of what his companions are doing.

Everyone must understand that rescue mode can only be maintained for a limited time period. Rescuers soon become tired, and they also become frustrated. The chance of a further accident becomes higher and higher, while at the same time the risk/benefit ratio is changing for the worse. For instance, the longer a victim is trapped underwater, the less likely they are to survive the rescue. This means there is less justifiable reason for the rescuers to continue in the risky rescue mode.

Operating in "Recovery Mode"

At some point during the rescue, you must shift out of "rescue mode" and into "recovery mode". Recovery mode is the response to use when the rescue is to recover equipment or bodies, and there is no justifiable reason for hasty or risky actions. One of the most difficult decisions you will ever make is deciding when to shift from rescue mode to recovery mode. If you are in the middle of trying to rescue a personal friend, and you decide that it is time to shift into recovery mode, you are in fact deciding that your friend has perished and there is little or no chance of his survival. Unfortunately, this decision must be made, because your own safety and the safety of the rest of your group will depend on it. The best recommendation that I can make is that rescue mode be initiated and maintained until you are sure that the victim has ceased to breathe for a period of one hour. After this time, there can be little realistic expectation of survival.

While it is easy to decide on a time limit of one hour, it may be considerably harder to define the point at which the victim actually stops breathing. There are any number of situations, especially in river canoeing, when a victim may be trapped, apparently underwater, and yet still be breathing sufficiently to provide a high chance of survival.

A number of years ago a friend of mine was visibly trapped against a strainer, completely underwater for 30 minutes. Everyone involved in the rescue believed that it was impossible for him to survive. However, the water flowing around his shoulders and head formed a small invisible pocket of air which allowed him to breathe enough to survive until he was finally pulled free.

Rescue priorities are also different from situation to situation. On an afternoon river trip, the loss of a canoe may not be a critically important problem. However, on a remote wilderness canoe trip, the loss of a canoe and provisions could spell disaster. In this situation the recovery of a canoe may be much more important in the assessment of the risk/benefit ratio.

When determining the risk/benefit ratio, and when deciding whether or not to operate in rescue mode, you must always keep in mind that the safety of the other members of the party is of paramount importance.

One thing that must be understood by canoeists, is that not all rescues are going to be successful. There may be times when you have all the right equipment, you perform all the necessary tasks, in fact, you do everything right, but the victim does not survive. This can be very difficult to accept if it happens to you. There are always extreme feelings of guilt, and the thoughts that there must have been something else you could have done. There probably wasn't. You do your best, you try as hard as you can, but you must understand that when you accept the inherent risks in canoeing, sometimes accidents will happen. The knowledge that you were fully prepared, and did the best that could have been done will help you to be able to deal with the loss of a paddler during an accident.

The Rescue Plan

The Goal of Safety & Rescue Training

In spite of the best pre-planning, unavoidable incidents can happen while you are canoeing. To be confident enough to organize and execute a successful rescue, you must have a wide repertoire of skills, and a prepared plan to put into action. The more practice and training you do, the more prepared you are, the more confident and successful you will be when an emergency arises.

Like most physical activities, you can't learn rescue skills solely from a book, so you must practice and accumulate your own experience. The goal of safety and rescue training, is to make the handling of emergency situations as routine as possible. An accident scene or emergency situation is not the place to attempt untried skills or procedures, or to experiment with new ideas. To do so would increase the risk of the planned rescue failing and possibly making a bad situation even worse. Successful rescue is not a result of spontaneous on-site improvisation. Rather it is the result of detailed pre-planning of emergency procedures.

A successful rescue begins long before the emergency occurs. It begins before you ever leave home. Your ability to effectively handle an emergency depends directly on the amount of pre-planning and organization you have done. Many people seem unwilling to face up to making contingency plans for disaster. They would much rather assume that accidents won't happen to them, or the weather won't change, or their equipment won't fail. However, unless you can anticipate the kind of problems you may be faced with, you cannot make suitable plans for dealing with them.

As a Paramedic, I face emergency situations every day. Every situation is unique, but if I had to think of a unique approach to each emergency call, I'd never be able to cope. Instead, we treat every accident in fundamentally the same way. This pre-planned approach is necessary because in an emergency, where rapid, critical decisions must be made, there is very limited time to actually think. There is certainly no time available to develop new thoughts. Paramedics, fire-fighters, and professional rescuers are successful because by applying a routine approach to every situation, they are assured that all steps are carried out in the appropriate order and priority. They choose appropriate techniques from a known repertoire of proven skills, and apply them to the current situation within the routine framework.

Whether you are a canoe tripper, a summer camp instructor, a professional guide, or a weekend paddler, your success as a rescuer will only be as good as the amount of time that you invest to learn and practice these safety and rescue skills. The middle of an emergency situation is no time to attempt a skill you have seen or practised only once or twice. Quick thinking, appropriate planning, and suitable resources, are all required to prevent a minor incident from turning into a major disaster.

Approaching the problem to carry out an accurate assessment.

TEN STEPS TO SUCCESSFUL RESCUE

1. Initial assessment.
2. Problem assessment.
3. Resource evaluation.
4. Develop rescue plan.
5. Delegate tasks.
6. Monitor/assess progress.
7. Re-assess, develop secondary plan.
8. Send for help.
9. First aid.
10. Evacuation.

Ten Steps to Successful Rescue

Over many years of dragging people and canoes out of rivers and lakes, I have come to realize that canoe rescue is no different from any other kind of emergency. You don't need to worry about how to deal with a great variety of rescue situations. By following 10 basic steps you will be able to deal with any situation, whether it is a simple capsize in a lake, or a catastrophe on a remote wilderness river.

The following ten steps outline the sequence of decisions and assessments that must be made during any rescue. See flowchart on page 126.

1. Initial Assessment

The first step, **initial assessment**, is critical. This is where you first realize that a problem does indeed exist. The sooner this happens the more likely a successful rescue can be made. This is also the time when you must first ensure your own safety and then ensure the safety of the rest of the group. Protecting people at an accident or rescue scene is an ongoing procedure, you should try to post at least one person to watch for the well being of the rescuers and the victim at all times.

On a lake, it can be very easy to lose sight of the victim during the initial assessment, and during the rescue. Your best chance of maintaining sight of the victim is to place a watcher on a high point overlooking the water. If the victim disappears, or the watcher loses track of him, it is important to always know the exact position where the victim was last seen. If at all possible the watcher should firmly fix this position in his mind using two or more in-line reference landmarks for the location. Protecting a river rescue scene may require one or two rescuers downstream of the scene with throw ropes, a rescue boat downstream of the site, and possibly a rescuer upstream of the scene to warn oncoming river traffic of the rescue in progress.

You should take these precautions at all times to ensure the continuing safety of the rescuers. Accidents commonly happen during practice sessions as people are learning new skills, working in unfamiliar surroundings, and experimenting with new techniques.

2. Problem Assessment

The next stage is for you to make an **assessment** of the nature and magnitude of the emergency. This includes determining whether the situation is stable, deteriorating, or fluctuating. At this time you must also make the initial determination of the risk/benefit ratio, and decide if the rescue is to be carried out in Rescue Mode or Recovery Mode.

3. Resource Evaluation

Before any actual rescue plans can be initiated you must not only make a considered evaluation of the situation, but must also **evaluate the resources** which are available. This will include the number of people and their skills, the amount of equipment that is immediately available, and what will be available in the near future.

4. Developing the Rescue Plan

Only when you have assessed both the problem and the resources, can you **develop a plan of action.** This is when the overall procedure and an outline of the techniques required to effect the rescue is decided upon.

The first stage of the plan of action should be one directed immediately towards stabilizing the situation and preventing further deterioration. For example, victims who are unable to help themselves, may require immediate hands-on support to prevent their heads from going under, and the situation from deteriorating. This is one case where the rescuers are at great risk, and even more so if they are not well trained. When you have a friend barely hanging on to a strainer, screaming for help with his head just above the surface, there is a tendency to overlook safety priorities. It can be very difficult trying to remember all the things that have to be done. This is when practice and training will help you to perform a successful rescue. Getting a rescuer to the victim may require paddling, swimming, fording, a tag line, or what ever is necessary to get a set of hands or a rope to the victim so he can be stabilized in place and his head kept above water.

While this initial stabilization will buy a little more time for you as a rescue leader, you must still continue with the development and execution of a definitive plan to complete the rescue, while doing your best to avoid personal hands-on involvement.

5. Delegation of Tasks

Once you have decided on the overall rescue plan, you must break it down into all the individual tasks that need to be carried out. You must then **delegate tasks** to the individuals or groups most able to successfully complete them.

6. Monitor/Assess Progress of the Rescue

Once the tasks are being carried out, and the plan is under way, you must **monitor and assess the progress** of the entire rescue. You must re-evaluate the risk/benefit ratio and closely monitor the situation to ensure the continued safety of the rescuers.

7. Re-assessment

As tasks are attempted or completed, and problems become more obvious, you must **reassess** the situation and your rescue plan. Make changes to the plan as necessary and possibly consider an alternative plan in case the first one fails, or in case the situation drastically changes.

8. Sending for Help

Calling for outside assistance, if necessary, is an important aspect of the rescue procedure. When and how you call for help depends on the distance to the nearest support services, the difficulty of the terrain, and the extent of your emergency. Calling for help is placed quite far down in the list of steps to rescue only because it is not consistently performed near the beginning of every rescue. There is no advantage in sending for help before you have all the information which will be required by a rescue agency.

When you send for help, it is important to specify as clearly as possible where you are located, what the problem is, the extent of injuries, what specific support you require, and your plans for completing the rescue. This information should include your plans for evacuating the victim to another location, or whether you plan to establish a camp and wait for further support.

9. First Aid

Whatever **first aid** is necessary must be administered to the patient as soon as possible. First aid might begin as soon as you can lay hands on the patient, and may continue until the patient has been evacuated to a hospital.

10. Evacuation

No rescue is complete until the victim is **evacuated** to an appropriate medical facility. This may be the longest and most difficult part of any rescue operation. The decisions you make about evacuation will depend on the condition of the patient, the resources of your group, and the distance to the nearest support facilities.

You must carry out all of these steps for a successful rescue, whether it is a simple capsize on a lake, or a complex river entrapment. Hopefully, the first five steps should be completed within the first 30 seconds to one minute after the accident happens. This is the time when the critical decisions must be made; when you must gather enough information to assess the risk/benefit ratio and decide what rescue techniques will need to be implemented.

MadRiverCanoe

4

Rescue Skills & Techniques

Canoes are usually very stable craft, which rarely capsize on calm water, or in good weather conditions. Mishaps usually happen in the middle of a rainstorm, in wind whipped waves, when you can barely see the other end of the canoe; it is in these situations where you need the experience and confidence to prevent a minor incident from escalating into a major disaster. It is, therefore, imperative that you practice rescue skills in a calm, controlled situation until you become skilled enough to function effectively under emergency conditions.

Choosing Appropriate Rescue Techniques

Which rescue technique you choose to apply during a rescue depends on the nature of the problem. You must use your knowledge and experience to choose the most appropriate rescue techniques in order to implement the quickest and safest rescue for the specific situation.

In any rescue, deciding which rescue techniques to use should always be done with due consideration of the rescue priorities. As always, your own safety comes first, after which you ensure that the site of the accident is made safe and others are protected.

In water rescue, it is imperative that everyone has at least a basic idea of your general rescue plan. A major problem of both river and lake incidents is that they can be very dynamic. Unlike other emergency situations, such as motor vehicle accidents, mountain rescues, or avalanche rescues, where events usually remain stable after the accident, water just keeps on moving.

It is easy to let the dynamics, excitement, and emotionally charged atmosphere of an emergency situation distract your attention from conducting a safe and efficient rescue unless you have a clear plan or basic framework for the rescue.

Your priorities in choosing the appropriate rescue techniques should follow the same guidelines for all water rescues. This is the **REACH, THROW, ROW, GO**, progression.

As your own safety and the safety of the other rescuers is paramount, a shore based (reach, throw) rescue should always be your first choice. Having your feet planted on firm ground will always be your safest position. If you have a throw rope or throwbag, and the terrain features are suitable, and time permits, this type of shore based reaching assist should be your first choice. It is easy to overlook this option if you are on the water in your canoe when someone capsizes. However, even if the victims are only a few metres upstream, you probably have time to get to shore, jump out with your throwbag, and perform the rescue. Only if this cannot be done safely should you attempt a canoe based

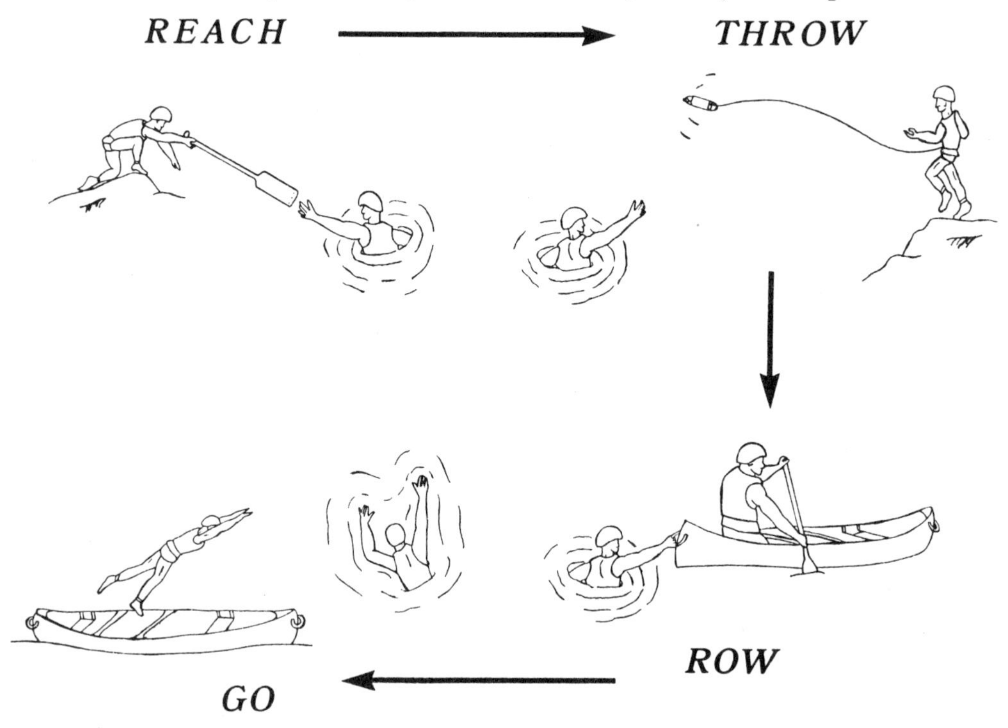

The sequence of REACH, THROW, ROW, GO, are the basic priorities of any water rescue.

rescue. Being out there in a canoe puts you at greater risk throughout the entire rescue. If a canoe based rescue fails, or is inappropriate, you may actually be forced to enter the water and perform a hands on rescue. This should be a last resort as it puts you, the rescuer, at the greatest risk of all.

If a victim or equipment is trapped or pinned, there will probably be technical/mechanical skills required to conduct the rescue. The decisions you make in choosing the most appropriate techniques must follow the same priority, that of minimizing risk to the rescuer. Always keep rescue techniques as simple as possible, and always progress from the lowest possible risk to rescuers, to higher levels of risk, according to your continuing assessment of the risk/benefit ratio. See flowchart page 127.

Skills Needed if You Capsize

What to Do if You Capsize

You aren't usually planning to capsize, and so when it occurs and you unexpectedly plunge into the cold water of a rapid or lake it is a shock and can also be a disorienting event. You will, however, function better if you have familiarized yourself ahead of time with the procedure you are going to follow. As a victim, you are an important participant in any rescue. The more you can help during the proceedings, the quicker and easier the rescue will be.

When a capsize occurs, there are a series of things which you must do to maximize the chance of a successful rescue, and minimize the chances of further injury to either you or to the rescuers.

The very first thing you should do is to hold onto your paddle. Once you let go of the paddle, you are unlikely to recover it yourself, which means that someone else will have to go and get it.

The second important step is to hold onto the canoe. The canoe supplies flotation and provides a very visible target for rescuers. If you are separated from your canoe, it can be extremely difficult for rescuers to keep track of your position in a set of rapids, or in rough water and poor weather conditions on a lake. If you maintain contact with your canoe, it means that the rescuers can recover both you and the canoe at the same time.

These first two steps are crucial, and must be done quickly. If you dump in a river, it is especially important that every effort in the rescue plan should be directed towards rescuing you and your equipment at the same time. Granted, you are the rescuers first concern, and ensuring your safety is their first priority. However, concentrating on you, while abandoning your equipment, may greatly complicate the rescue. It means more time, manpower, and risk is involved in first recovering you, then your gear, and then reuniting you with your gear. This can put the rescuers at far more risk than may have been necessary. Whenever possible, hang on to your paddle and canoe so that you can be rescued all at one time.

After a capsize, the third priority for you is to breathe. When you are unexpectedly plunged into freezing cold water, this may not be as easy as it sounds. It is difficult to stay relaxed. The reaction to the cold water, or initially choking on a mouthful of water, or both, can easily lead to fear and panic which will work against the required steady breathing. It will require firm self control on your part to remain calm and concentrate on your breathing under these conditions.

On a lake, the next step is to provide whatever help and assistance your partner may need. Once the equipment is under control, and you are all in a safe position, the rescue can continue.

In a river rescue there are more steps for you to carry out after a capsize before you look to your partner. Once you have hold of your canoe and paddle, it is time for you to move to the upstream end of the canoe. It doesn't matter which end, as long as it is the upstream end. You must never end up downstream of the canoe because of the possibility of being crushed between the canoe and an obstacle. If the canoe touches the bottom, or is hitting obstacles, it may be spun around many times in the current. You may have to be continuously on the move to stay upstream of the canoe.

Once you are at the upstream end, you must assumes a position where you have the canoe in one hand, the paddle in the other. You should be on your back facing downstream, with your feet at the surface. In this position you can see what is coming, can fend off any obstacles with your feet, and you can try to keep the canoe as parallel to the current as possible.

Once you are in this position at the upstream end of the canoe, on your back with your feet downstream, you are in the best position to protect yourself from further injury. ONLY NOW is it time for you to take a look and check on the safety of your partner. This is because protecting yourself is always your first priority. If you become injured, you compound the problem, as well as being unable to help your partner.

If your partner is in need of assistance or support, you must get him into the same protective position at the upstream end of the canoe as quickly as possible.

While in this position, your main objective is to try as best you can to keep the canoe as parallel to the current as possible. This helps to keep you at the upstream end, and also presents the smallest profile of the canoe to any obstacles downstream, minimizing the chances of a the canoe being wrapped sideways around an obstacle or "broaching".

As I have mentioned, it is **always** best to stay with your canoe whenever possible. Staying with the canoe is a safe option if the water temperature permits, and help is likely to come. In choosing this option, you need to be certain that help in the form of other paddlers in the group, or people on shore will arrive. The canoe itself will always provide extra flotation. It also provides a very visible marker to other rescuers, which can be important in rough water and poor visibility. When there is only one canoe present, your options for rescue are very limited indeed. For you to successfully swim an open canoe full of water to shore, in a lake, or in any kind of a current, is a near impossibility and cannot be counted on as a viable rescue procedure.

However, there are times when leaving your canoe is certainly indicated. On a lake, remaining in very cold water for any length of time can quickly lead to your being incapacitated. If there is no chance of rescuers arriving in short order, you may have to leave the canoe and try to reach shore.

In a river, the victim should be at the upstream end of the canoe, on his back, with feet at the surface.

The victims are an important component of a successful rescue, and must be aware and alert of the rescue attempts which are going on around them.

If, on a river, you and the canoe are heading for obvious danger, such as a strainer or a waterfall, this is the time to abandon the canoe and strike out on your own. The same may be true if you are on an unknown river. If you don't know what is around the bend, it may be better to get to shore while you still can.

Once you have completed these initial steps after your capsize, you must be alert and aware of the rescue proceedings which are going on around you. You should already know what rescue techniques are going to be used, and be looking for the throw rope, or rescue boat, and be listening for instructions.

HELP Position

If you have to wait around in the cold water of a lake, it is necessary to minimize your heat loss as much as possible because cold water will quickly incapacitate you. One way to do this is to assume the "Heat Escape Lessening Position" (HELP position) while waiting for assistance to arrive. Floating in the HELP position will allow you to stay as warm as possible for as long as possible.

The HELP position is similar to a fetal position. The arms are held in close to the body to prevent heat loss from the sides and armpits, with the hands pressed up to the neck to reduce water circulation around the great blood vessels in this area. The legs are held tightly together and flexed to reduce heat loss from the groin and insides of the thighs.

In cold water, the HELP position will let you stay as warm as possible for as long as possible.

Huddle Position

If there are three swimmers, a similar position called the HUDDLE position can be utilized. This position is similar to the HELP position except that the victims form a circle with arms interlocked or tightly across each others shoulders. It has the same effect as the HELP position and also reduces the water circulation around the entire group by maintaining a pool of still water inside the circle.

How to Use the Canoe for Extra Flotation

If there are two of you, the canoe itself can be used as a flotation device and to assist in maintaining warmth. One of you should get on each side of the overturned canoe at the midpoint. Face each other, cross your arms over the canoe and clasp each others hands. The canoe will support your upper bodies, holding you much higher out of the water than does a PFD alone. Your legs should be flexed and your knees drawn up inside the canoe. This position keeps your legs warmer by reducing the water circulation around them. The more you can keep your body out of the water, the warmer you will be because water conducts heat away from you about 30 times faster than air.

If you are in moving water, you cannot use these techniques and must move to the upstream end of the canoe. Hanging on to the end loop, you can still use the canoe as an extra flotation device, but you must not be in a position downstream of the canoe where the potential may exist of being caught between the canoe and an obstacle in the river.

The cross arm over canoe technique pulls you higher out of the water, provides extra flotation and helps keep you warm.

Swimming to Shore

Unfortunately, floating around with the canoe, in a lake or river, doesn't do much for you. Sooner or later you are somehow going to have to continue the rescue.

If the water is very cold, and no one is likely to come out to rescue you, swimming to shore may be a viable option. Hopefully, when you are paddling on a lake you will be close enough to shore that if you capsize, you will be able to swim the distance before you are incapacitated by cold or fatigue. Swimming to the shore of a lake should be done carefully and slowly to conserve your energy and reduce fatigue. In rough water and poor weather it may be very difficult to even see the shore from the surface of the water, and you must make continuous efforts to remain correctly oriented to the direction of the shore.

After a river capsize, you will have to swim to shore if you are alone, or if there are any dangerous obstacles downstream that you must avoid before rescuers can get to you.

If you lose contact with the canoe during the capsize, you will end up free swimming in the river. Free swimming in rapids should be done on the back with the feet downstream. This allows you to see where you are going and where the obstructions are. A back stroking action with the arms should be used to control your position and maneuver in the rapids. If there is a hazard downstream, and you do have to move somewhere in a hurry, you should let go of your paddle, turn over, and use the normal crawl stroke. It is a less safe way of swimming, and you would only use the crawl to get away from an even more serious danger.

Hazards when Swimming in Rivers

When free swimming in a set of rapids, you have little control over the line you take; you are going where the current wants to take you. Unfortunately, the current may be going directly into a strainer. This is one of the most dangerous situations to be in, and if this does happen, you must prevent yourself from being pushed under the strainer and pinned there by the current. The only way to avoid being pinned, is for you to turn around so that you are facing downstream towards the strainer. You must then swim as hard as possible, and with a powerful kicking motion, jump, climb, and pull yourself up and over the strainer. You may not get right over the strainer, but at least you have a chance to get as high on it as possible to where you can hang on with your head above the water. If you wait until you hit the strainer to get organized, it will be far too late. You will probably be pushed underneath and pinned there underwater until someone comes to get you out. In reality, getting you out may require the dismantling of a log-jam, and is almost sure to be a body recovery rescue.

If you are still upright in the canoe, and are heading for an unavoidable strainer, you should first turn your canoe broadside to the strainer so that if there are two of you, you both have the chance to get out. Just before you hit the strainer you both jump out, up and towards, or over the strainer. The objective is to get as much of your body as possible out of the water and on top of the strainer where you can hang on until help arrives.

Do not take chances with strainers. Abandon your equipment, even abandon your partner if you must, just don't get pinned underneath a strainer. There is usually no way out that is quick enough to save your life. This is one of the times when the risk/benefit ratio is just too disadvantageous to justify any attempt at direct hands-on rescue of a victim. If one paddler disappears under a log jam, it is suicidal to send another paddler under the log jam to try and get him out.

The other hazard to avoid while swimming in rapids is having a foot or ankle become wedged between two rocks. You can reduce the possibility of this by keeping your feet well up off the bottom of the river while swimming, and waiting until the water is really shallow and slow before trying to stand up.

How to Get a Swamped Canoe to Shore

Some paddlers carry a long line while lake paddling to help them bring the canoe to shore. If you carry a 5-6 mm line, 50-100 metres long, you can attach one end of the line to the canoe, swim to shore with the other end, and then pull the canoe to shore. If you always stay within 50-100 metres of shore, this method will work most of the time.

If you have capsized on a river, it is a near impossibility to swim an open canoe full of water to shore in any kind of a current. Swimming the canoe to shore in this case cannot be counted on as a viable rescue procedure. You must usually swim to shore, and then retrieve the canoe and equipment as best you can.

One option when paddling alone is to use a rope for self retrieval of the canoe. One end of the rope is permanently secured to the bow or stern of the canoe. The rest of the rope is loosely stored, with the other end fixed for quick release. When the canoe capsizes, you grab the free end of the rope, swim to shore, then pull in the swamped canoe. You can also use a throwbag to achieve the same result. While paddling, the rope loop handle of the throwbag is clipped to the end of the canoe. When you capsize, you grab the throwbag itself and swim to shore. While you swim, the rope pays out of the throwbag, and upon reaching shore, you pull in the canoe.

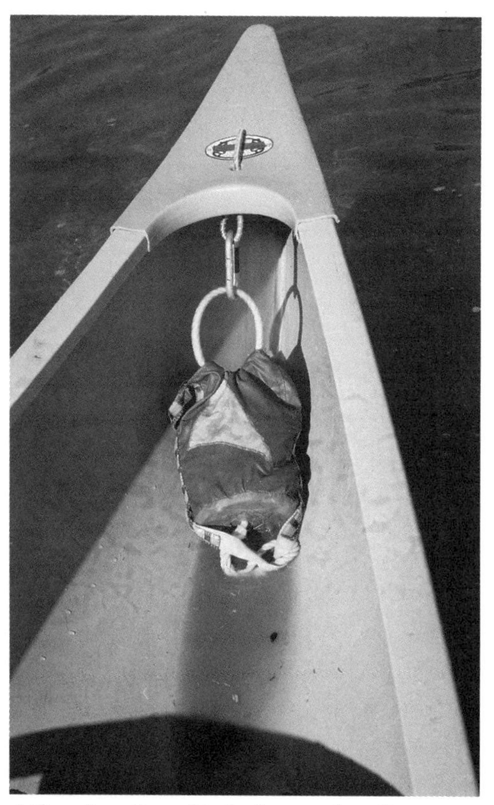

A throwbag clipped in by the rope handle is ready for self rescue.

While these techniques do work, they have severe limitations. Your rope must be long enough to reach shore and there must be no obstacles downstream between the canoe and shore which could catch the rope while you are swimming. The shore must also be suitable, both for you to get out, and then clear enough for you to move along as you swing the canoe into the bank.

Another problem is that you may be moving downstream more slowly than the canoe once you enter the slower water near to shore. If you do not get to shore soon enough, you will find yourself being dragged downstream and unable to get you or your canoe to shore. However, even with these limitations, this technique is probably the best chance a single canoeist has of retrieving a swamped canoe in a set of rapids. It is much easier if the canoe has full buoyancy and is therefore not as full of water and not as heavy.

How to Paddle a Swamped Canoe

Paddling the swamped canoe to shore is another option. To perform this skill you and your partner climb into the swamped canoe, at the same time and from opposite sides. Once inside, sit on the floor of the canoe, with your legs straight out in front. This lowers your centre of gravity and allows the canoe to float as high as possible, raising your upper bodies and arms above the surface. Using your paddles or your hands, you can then paddle to shore. Although awkward in appearance, this method does move the canoe fairly well,

A capsized canoe can be paddled to shore.

and you can travel a good distance. Having extra flotation in your canoe makes this technique much more efficient. Paddling the canoe to shore also keeps you and the canoe together so you always have the support of the canoe's flotation if you need to rest. This technique can also be used when river paddling if you end up in the calm water at the bottom of a set of rapids. In this case paddling your swamped canoe to shore may be the easiest and quickest method of rescue. This technique also works well for the solo paddler.

One thing that severely hampers paddling a swamped canoe is the presence of packs or gear attached to the canoe. It is usually more effective to untie the packs and leave them. Once you arrive at shore, you can empty the canoe and paddle back out to get the gear. However, wind and water conditions may make it unwise to abandon your gear. If you choose not to leave the gear, the packs should be brought inside the canoe with you. This allows for the most efficient movement of the canoe through the water.

Righting, Emptying, and Re-Entering the Canoe while in the Water

Righting and emptying a swamped canoe while still in the water, is probably the quickest and most efficient way to effect a rescue. One way to do this is to use the "throwover" technique. Also known as the Capistrano flip, or the Canoe Toss, it is a quick way of righting and emptying a swamped canoe. A two person skill, the basic technique is that the paddlers get underneath the swamped canoe, and throw it up in the air so that the canoe rights itself and empties itself at the same time. Accomplishing this skill is actually much easier than it may sound. The first step in carrying out a throwover is to ensure that the swamped canoe is clear of all gear.

First turn the canoe if necessary, so that it is floating bottom up. Then make your way, one to each end of the canoe. Duck under the canoe so that you have your heads up inside the canoe, facing each other with your hands on the gunnels. Once in the airspace underneath the canoe, you can easily talk to each other and co-ordinate your movements. First decide on which side of the canoe you are going to push upwards. Tilt the canoe slightly away from that side to break the vacuum seal between the gunnels and the water. Support the opposite gunnel with one hand, and while giving a powerful scissor kick with your legs, you both thrust the other gunnel straight up in the air. Done properly, you are forced underwater, while the canoe will flip right over and be upright, completely empty of water. This is a simple technique and easily mastered with practice. I have seen very small people perform this skill quite successfully and it seems to work on any type of canoe. Even if the canoe doesn't completely empty itself, it should at least have lost enough water to maintain freeboard while you bail out the remainder. While primarily a flat water skill, the throwover could be applied to rivers in some situations, such as being in a deep water eddy with only steep banks or cliffs surrounding you.

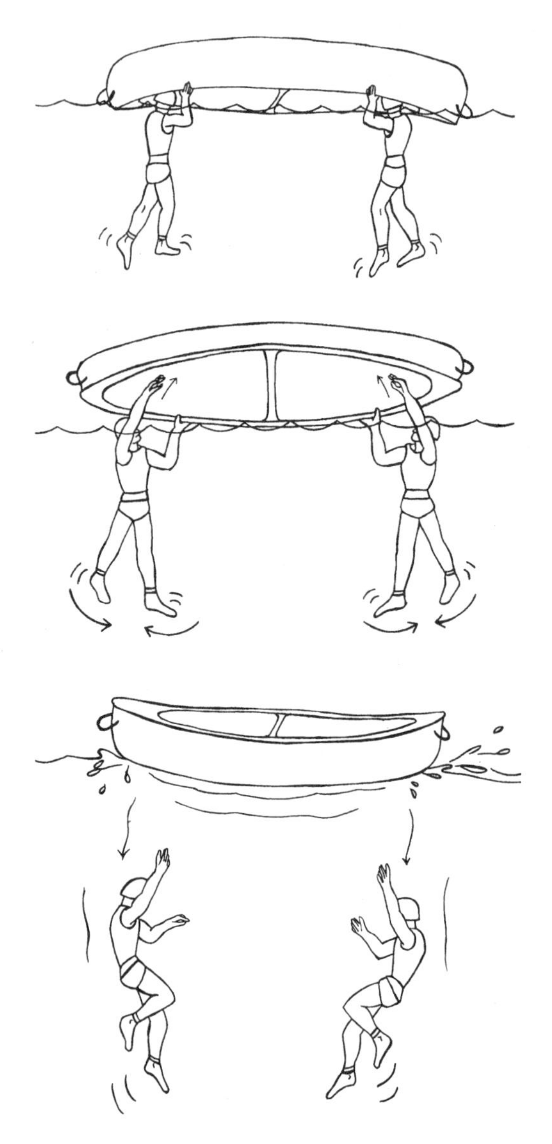

Once the canoe is upright and empty, it is very important to keep hold of it. An empty canoe is easily blown out of reach by even a light breeze. If you do have gear tied to the canoe with an appropriate tie in rope, the packs will act as a sea anchor for the canoe while you prepare to get back in. If not, it is wise to hold a painter in your hand before you perform the throwover.

How to Get Into an Empty Canoe from Deep Water

Being able to get into a canoe from deep water is a necessary skill for all paddlers. The most difficult situation is when you must climb into an empty canoe on your own. There are two main ways to do this. The first is to approach the side of the canoe, **just in front of the stern seat**. Grasping the gunnel, give a strong scissor kick while reaching up and across the canoe to place one hand on the far gunnel. In this position you can use one hand on each gunnel to stabilize the canoe. With another strong kick, you then pull your hips above the level of the gunnel. At this point you should be laying face down across the gunnels of the canoe. Now you only have to roll over on your back and allow your hips to fall into the canoe to be safely sitting in a dry canoe.

An alternative method is to approach the side of the canoe closer to the midthwart, reaching over the gunnels with your hands and arms. A strong kick should allow you to place your hands directly in the bottom of the tumblehome of the canoe. In this position you can press straight down, tilting the gunnel toward you, but not capsizing the canoe. Another strong kick and downward push with the arms should allow you to bring your shoulders, then your hips across the gunnel. Once your hips cross the gunnel, a forward sideways roll should deliver you on your back in the bottom of the canoe.

If there are two of you in the water you can help each other, making it much easier to re-enter the canoe. To do this, first get on opposite sides of the canoe. One of you hangs onto the gunnel, stabilizing the canoe, while the other climbs in from the other side. The climbing in, as described above, is easier if your partner stabilizes the canoe after raising the gunnel on their side, thus bringing the opposite gunnel right down to the level of the water. This allows you to climb directly into the canoe without having to pull yourself up over a high gunnel. Once inside the canoe, you then stabilize the canoe by leaning, so that your partner can climb in.

A single paddler should be able to get back into an empty canoe.

Two paddlers in the water can assist each other in getting back into the canoe.

Skills for the Rescuer to Use from the Shore

In any water rescue operation, your safest position as a rescuer is to have both feet planted firmly on land and to conduct the rescue from shore. When possible, using a "reaching assist" will be the best way to retrieve the victims. This may mean reaching with a paddle or branch. A canoe with two painters tied together may let you reach up to 10 metres out into the water. A reaching assist may also mean throwing the victim some form of flotation device to help him stay afloat until you can organize some other type of rescue. However, unless the victims are very close to shore, your best tool for a reaching assist is going to be a coil of rope or a throwbag.

How to Throw a Coil of Rope

To accurately throw a coil of rope over any distance is a skill requiring a good deal of practice. It is best not to try and throw too much rope, at least not when you are first learning. With experience, 30 metres is probably the maximum you will be able to handle, and still count on some degree of accuracy.

The easiest method is to start with a smoothly coiled length of rope, with the coils medium sized, about 70-80 cm diameter. Hold on to the shore end of the rope. I usually put my foot on it to make sure it doesn't follow the thrown rope. Split the coils into two even halves, holding one half firmly in your throwing hand, and leaving the other half loosely held in the other. In between the coils should be enough loose rope to allow you full swing of your throwing arm. The rope can be thrown under handed or with a side arm motion. As the first coil leaves your hand, allow the second half of the coils to feed freely and smoothly off your other hand. If you do miss with your first throw, you can quickly recoil the rope and try again. To be able to throw a rope consistently and accurately by this method requires extensive and constant practice. However it does allow you to make better use of your safety line.

A coil of rope split into two parts in preparation for throwing. Not shown is his foot standing on the loose end

How to Use a Throwbag

An easier way to throw a rescue rope is to use a throwbag. Using a throwbag is relatively simple, but does require practice. The more you practice, the better you will be. Pick up the throwbag by the webbing handle with your throwing hand. The other hand grasps the rope handle, and a quick jerk frees the rope and you are ready to go. The way you actually throw the rope is a matter of personal preference, and may depend on the type of throwbag you are using. You can throw underhand like pitching a softball, overhand like throwing a knife, or overhand like tossing a football. All can work equally well with practice.

Before throwing a throwbag or throw rope, make sure that you first have the victim's attention. This may seem unnecessary, but too many times I've seen throwbags land all around a victim and be totally ignored. When a victim first capsizes, he is very busy, looking after his gear, getting into position, and assisting his

With the rope loop held in one hand, and the bag held in the other hand, the throwbag is ready to be thrown.

partner. There is no point in tossing a throwbag if the victim is not ready to receive it, or not paying attention to you. It is best to first shout "rope", then try to make eye contact with the victim so that you know he is paying attention and looking towards you.

When throwing a throwbag into a river it is best to aim directly at the victim. If the rope lands upstream of the victim, it is unlikely to float down to him, since the victim and the throwbag are floating at the same speed. If it lands downstream, the victim may not be able to see it or find it in the water. You want to practice enough so that you are reasonably accurate with whatever device you use.

In river rescues, the type of shoreline will affect your ability to control, hold and land a victim, and will dictate whether or not a throwbag should be used. Once a victim grabs onto the end of the rope, it soon becomes taut, and you will be holding against the entire force of the current pushing on the victim and his equipment. In a moderate current, and if you are only rescuing the victim, you can probably hold onto him just by bracing yourself, and keeping a firm grip on the rope. If however, the victim has a canoe with him, holding on is much more difficult for both the rescuer and the victim. Once the victim and the canoe reach the end of a tight rope, the forces build immediately. If you try and hold tightly to the rope, the forces will become too great and one of three things will happen. Either the victim will let go of the rope, or the victim will let go of the canoe, or the rescuer will go water-skiing! Although you may be able to tie off or belay the rope, the victim can only hang on with one-handed grip strength. Therefore the rescuer must move down the shoreline to create a very dynamic belay so that the forces do not become more than the victim can handle. In order to best judge the stress on the victim, you should hold onto the throwbag handle with only one hand. This way, you can feel the same forces as the victim, and be able to determine when they are reaching unacceptable levels. The best way to effectively retrieve the victim is to move along the shore, pulling in the victim and the canoe a bit at a time. To do this requires a relatively clear shoreline where you can move downstream easily without worrying about rocks, roots, or trees. The downstream ends of islands, on small points of land, from the top of steep banks, and from individual boulders, are all poor choices of places from which to throw a rope because you have nowhere to move.

Another consideration in positioning yourself to use a throwbag, is where on the shore the victim is going to arrive as he pendulums in on the end of the rope. There must be no obstructions downstream and inshore of the victims when the rope is thrown because they may get caught in the rope as the victims pendulum into shore. There is also no advantage in swinging a victim in from the centre of the river, to a position along a steep bank with swift current where it is not suitable for him to get out of the river. If this happens, the victim will probably have to let go of the rope and become free floating once again. He may now be upstream of a dangerous obstacle, such as a strainer, and your rescue attempt has made the situation worse instead of better.

Reaching assists and shore based rescue may be your only available option if the situation is very dangerous. A decision to use these methods will be dictated by your assessment of the risk/

benefit ratio. There may be times when the risk/benefit ratio is just too disadvantageous to justify any attempt at hands on, or boat based, rescue of the victim. The most common example of this is rescue from a hydraulic. When a paddler is trapped in a powerful hydraulic at the base of a low head dam, or in a naturally occurring hydraulic on a river, he may be absolutely unable to escape on his own. However, there is often simply no safe way for another paddler to perform a hands on, or boat based rescue either. In these situations the only safe procedure is to try and get a rope or some other reaching assist to the victim from the shore. If this is impossible, the only alternative is to closely monitor the situation and hope that something changes. Technical weir rescue requires highly specialized boats, equipment, and training if it is to be performed with any degree of safety to the rescuers. This must be left to professional responders such as those fire departments or dive rescue agencies which have undergone specific water rescue training. Any attempt at in-water weir rescue with inadequate equipment or improperly trained rescuers is probably only going to result in the loss of more lives.

Skills and Techniques for River Crossing

River crossing is a fundamental skill required for river rescue. Whether you are ferrying a canoe across, making your way to a victim, moving gear across, setting up a traverse line, or retrieving a pinned canoe, you are always dealing with crossing the river.

For shallow water crossings, or crossing where a canoe is unavailable, there are a number of techniques which can be used.

Swimming

Swimming across a river may be safer than trying to walk on an uneven river bed, and it may be your only choice if the river is too deep to ford. For swimming, it is best to choose a deep, narrow channel, with good eddies on both sides, and no immediate hazards anywhere downstream. This should allow you to get across with the least amount of downstream movement. Swim facing upstream, using a forward crawl, just like ferrying a canoe. If you have to swim a rope across a river, always use the smallest diameter rope possible because any rope creates tremendous drag as soon as it is in a current. A thin rope can easily be used to later draw a thicker rope across the river.

Wading

Your ability to successfully cross a river on foot depends on the speed and depth of the water. Since speed is the critical factor, even very shallow water may be impossible to cross on foot if it is flowing very fast. The only way to judge what speed of water you can safely cross is by experience. The more you practice river crossing, the more confidently and accurately you will be able to assess river currents. Remember, one of the main hazards in wading rivers is the potential for foot entrapment.

It is best to attempt a foot crossing at a place where the water is as slow and shallow as possible. When crossing by yourself, always try to use a paddle or branch as an additional support. Facing upstream so that the pressure of the water locks your knees, use the paddle for support and move your feet across. Once your feet are firmly in place, move the paddle across. In this way you can make your way across the river, moving from eddy to eddy.

Using a branch or paddle makes a shallow crossing much easier.

Wading with People for Support

Two or three people crossing together can increase stability and cross faster water than one person can. Two people stand, facing each other, with their hands on each others shoulders. The upstream person stays braced and stationary. This forms an eddy immediately downstream, where the second person is standing. Once the downstream person has moved across this eddy, he then braces the upstream person so that they in turn can move, and so on across the river.

Paddlers can use each other for support to make a shallow water crossing.

Three people can move in a similar fashion. Forming a tripod with their hands on each others shoulders, they travel with a co-ordinated rotational movement to cross the current.

Wading with the Assistance of a Rope

Ropes can be used in various ways to assist in river crossings, but because of the hydraulic forces which are developed in moving water, rescuers should never be put into any position where they cannot instantly release themselves from a rope system. **It is a fundamental rule of river rescue that no one is ever tethered or tied to a rope in moving water.** Anytime a rescuer or victim need to use a rope it should be hand held only. If he needs to use his hands, the rope should be carried by means of a large loop, at least a metre in diameter, worn across one shoulder. This will always allow the person to release the rope when necessary. There are also specialized harnesses or belts available which serve the same purpose. They allow a rope to be securely fastened to the rescuer, leaving his hands free to work, but they also have a quick release buckle to instantly detach the system.

A Pendulum Crossing

When a rope is available, you may be able to use it to assist you in a pendulum crossing. The longer the rope, the better — preferably at least twice the width of the river. One end of the rope is fixed to shore as far upstream of the crossing site as possible. Hold onto the downstream end of the rope, and make your way across the river in a pendulum motion, using tension on the rope as support against the force of the current. As long as the angle between the rope and the current stays reasonably small, the rope provides excellent support against the current. This system can allow you to cross a much stronger current than would be possible without a rope.

A rope fastened upstream can allow a paddler to make a pendulum crossing.

Because the upstream support from the rope decreases the farther out from shore you travel, it is always best to use this technique to cross from an area of fast current to an area of slower current. This means that you have less pressure on you from the current at the same time that you have less support from the rope.

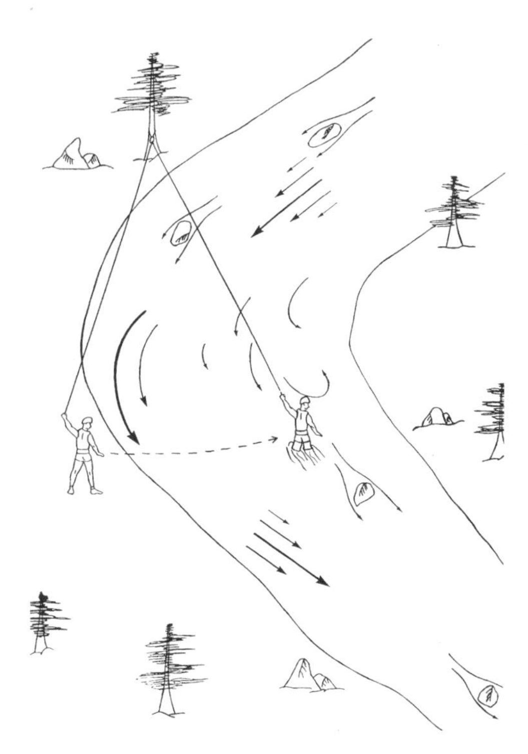

A curve or bend in the river may be the best place to use this technique. By anchoring the upstream end of the rope along a bend, you can achieve the greatest amount of support for the longest distance across the river.

A Rope Traverse Crossing

If a large number of people or many crossings are required, and the equipment is available, it may be worth setting up a fixed rope across the river to use as a rope traverse (see page 92, Rigging a Rope Across a River). For a rope traverse, the rope is stretched as taut as possible across the river and is used as a supportive handrail by people wading across.

If the river is to be crossed in both directions, the rope is best set at right angles to the current. The area chosen should be as shallow as possible so that the rescuers can stand upright in the current, using the rope mostly for balance. The traverse rope must be kept as tight as possible, usually about one metre above the surface. If the rope is not tight enough, it will "V" downstream, making the rescuer work upstream against the current from the middle of the rope to reach the far side.

If the river crossing is going to be in one direction only, the traversing rope can be set at an angle of 30-40 degrees to the shore. If the rope is kept tight enough, the current will assist the rescuer across the river. In deeper water, the rescuer can clip a carabiner and a sling into the angled traversing rope. Holding onto this sling with his hand, the rescuer can then be swept quickly and easily across the river.

Using a traverse rope to make a river crossing.

Skills for a Rescuer to Use from on the Water

If you are too far from shore for a reaching assist to be practical, or if the victims are unable to grasp the rope, you will have to attempt a boat based rescue. Approaching a victim in your canoe, or attempting any kind of boat based rescue, does put you at greater risk and therefore any water-based rescue must be well thought out and carefully controlled to minimize the risk.

Performing a T-Rescue

The quickest and most efficient way to recover a swamped canoe is to perform a T-rescue. This is a simple procedure, and once perfected can be applied in many situations.

To perform this skill, paddle up to the closest end of the swamped canoe. Bring your canoe at right angles to the swamped canoe, with the bow of the capsized canoe at the middle of your canoe, forming the "T". The swamped canoe must be empty of gear to allow a T-rescue, or the gear must be tied in as previously described, with a rope at least one half the length of the canoe. If there are two of you in the canoe, one person usually performs the T-rescue while the other one stabilizes your canoe and keeps track of the victims. It is often best for the bowman to perform the rescue. This way the sternsman has a clear view of the procedure and can provide any assistance necessary .

The bowman first turns around in the bow seat, facing the stern, and grabs onto the end of the overturned canoe. The end of the overturned canoe is then lifted up onto the gunnel of your canoe. If the capsized canoe is fully upright or completely upside down, it may make the lifting a little easier to first turn the canoe onto its side especially as a partial vacuum forms if all the gunwales are under water. Once the bow of the canoe is across your gunnel, the canoe is turned completely upside down and slid 90° across your canoe until it is completely free of the water. Then, lifting one side of the canoe, you turn it

completely upright again, and slide it back into the water. Now you can put the gear back in, then assist the victims back into their own canoe. The T-rescue can still be very useful even if you do not manage, or have sufficient time, to pull the canoe completely free of the water across your gunnels. Even a partially complete T-rescue will remove the majority of the water from the swamped canoe.

In order to perform the T-rescue successfully, it is necessary to make sure that your canoe gunnels and those of the rest of the group, are clear. Gear such as fishing poles or paddles sticking up above the gunnels will interfere with the T-rescue.

The T-rescue is a basic skill which can be applied in many different ways. For example, it can be performed by victims in the water with two swamped canoes. In this situation, one of the victims stabilizes one of the capsized canoes upside down in the water, trapping as much air underneath as possible. This overturned canoe will provide sufficient support to T-rescue the other canoe. The second victim then reaches across the centre of the stabilized canoe, grabbing the painter or end loop of the other canoe. He then pulls the canoe upside down, across the centre of the stabilized canoe. Once the canoe is half way across and empty, it is turned over and slid back into the water. Two victims can then get back into the upright canoe, and T-rescue the remaining canoe.

Similarly, if there is only one canoe, it is quite possible to perform a T-rescue by pulling the swamped canoe across the gear bags. A couple of large packs have enough flotation to allow at least a partial T-rescue. By this means the canoe may not end up completely empty, but should allow you to get in while maintaining clear freeboard, and you can bail out the rest of the water.

The T-rescue can be very useful in river rescues, but you must consider what is downstream before you put yourself at risk. Although T-rescues can be performed in rapids with very big waves and fast water, if there are numerous rocks, or constant maneuvering is necessary, a T-rescue may simply be too dangerous for the rescuers to attempt.

To perform a T-rescue in the river you should always approach the capsized canoe towards the upstream end. This should bring you to the victims and the canoe at the same time. Once the victims are securely holding onto the ends of your canoe, you can proceed with the rescue. The critical factor in a successful T-rescue on a river is speed. The dangerous period for the rescuer is while the capsized canoe is being pulled from the water, across the gunnels and turned over. At this time the rescue canoe has no maneuverability at all. With practice, you should be able to perform this skill within 10 seconds of the time you lay hands on the end of the canoe. Once you have the canoe across your gunnels, turned upright so the ends don't catch in the water, the rescue canoe is free to move. At this point you can toss the victims gear bag into your canoe, and paddle quite normally. If you are just rescuing the canoe by itself, it may be much easier to paddle the canoe to shore in this position, rather than try to put it in the water and tow it to shore. You might also have your partner get into the rescued canoe, and you both paddle solo to shore.

However, if the victims are with you, the canoe should be put back in the water, and the victims can then be assisted back into their canoe.

After a T-rescue an empty canoe can be quickly and easily paddled to shore without putting it back in the water.

Towing a Swamped Canoe to Shore

It may be impossible to perform a T-rescue. If the capsized canoe has the gear tied directly to the thwarts, or if the canoe is equipped with a spray deck, or if you dealing with closed deck canoes, a T-rescue will not work. In this case your only option may be to tow the canoe to shore.

When towing a canoe, especially in a river, you want to ensure that you can instantly release yourself if the need should arise. A simple way to do this is to take the painter of the capsized canoe, and wrap it two to three times around the stern thwart of your canoe, and put your foot on the free end. To release the tow, you simply take your foot off the rope.

Another method is to tie the painter to your thwart with an unfinished or slipped, clove hitch. To release the tow, just pull the knot free.

If you spend a lot of time performing rescues during instructional courses, or paddle with closed canoes, you may want to rig a permanent system for towing on your canoe. One way to do this is to mount a sailing jam cleat on your deck. A tow line is locked in the jam cleat, and the line is stored under a bungie cord with a carabiner attached to the trailing end of the rope. When you want to

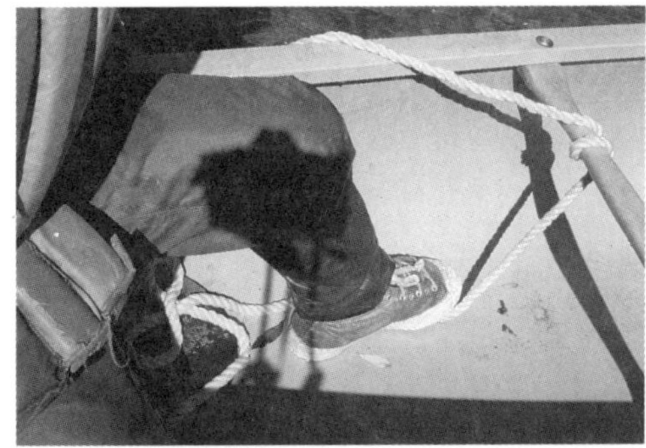

A painter can be wrapped around your thwart to tow a capsized canoe.

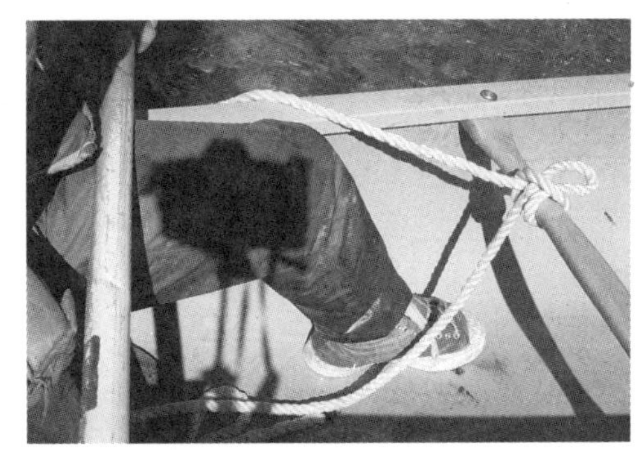

A slipped clove hitch allows quick release during a tow.

A quick release towing system mounted on the stern deck of the canoe.

tow, just grab the carabiner and clip it into the painter or end loop of the capsized canoe. To release the tow, simply pull the rope out of the jam cleat. This type of system is quite versatile as it does not require the capsized canoe to be equipped with a painter.

If you are going to tow a canoe in a river you must ensure that are there are no serious obstructions immediately downstream. Towing in a river is usually accomplished with the stern of the rescue canoe at the upstream end of the capsized canoe, in the forward ferry position. The victim(s) hold onto the end of the capsized canoe and the stern of the rescue canoe, while you perform a forward ferry, towing the victims and their canoe to shore. During this process, you must be continuously alert for obstructions and hazards downstream as you will be progressing downstream backwards with little maneuverability. In difficult rapids, where clear visibility is critical to the rescue, it may not be safe for you to tow the victims directly to shore in the upstream (forward) ferry position. In this case, keep your canoe facing downstream, with the victims holding onto the stern of the rescue canoe. Tow them through the rapids until a suitable place is reached where you can turn your canoe and tow the victims to shore. Downstream towing is a dangerous maneuvre for you to undertake as it puts you directly downstream of the victims and their canoe.

Towing a capsized canoe is hard work, and not a quick process. There will be significant downstream movement during the tow, and if you approach a hazard, you must be prepared to instruct the victims to let go of the capsized canoe. You will then have to tow just the victims to shore as quickly as possible.

If the victims are not with the canoe, then you must have some system available to tow the capsized canoe. Any of the previously described systems will work, but it is especially important that there always be a way for the rescuers to quickly release the capsized canoe.

Skills to Assist Victims in the Water

Whenever possible, I avoid allowing any victims into my canoe during a rescue. If the victims of an accident are active and uninjured, the best place for them to be is in the water. People getting into your canoe can be a very unstabilizing influence, reducing your freeboard and decreasing your own safety. I also require the victims to control their own gear, including their paddles. The first thing people in the water seem to want to do, is swim up to you and put their paddles into your canoe. This only clutters up your canoe, makes it more difficult to move about, and separates the victims from their gear that they will need once they are back in their own canoe.

The first step is to make sure that the victims need no immediate help and that they can follow directions. I usually find it best to send them to hang onto the ends of my canoe. This places them out of the way of rescue operations. Also, if they pull down on the ends of my canoe, it doesn't interfere with my stability like it does if they are along side and pull down. Being at the ends also makes it more difficult for the victims to decide to climb into my canoe when I am not looking.

Assisting a victim from a kneeling position in the canoe.

If the victims are injured, or need immediate assistance for any reason, you must deal with them right away. This may mean giving them a flotation device of some sort, holding their head above water, or even beginning resuscitation. Dealing with a victim in the water, from a canoe, can be difficult. There are two positions which work well. One is to kneel in the centre of the canoe, with both your knees right in the tumblehome, at one side of the canoe. This position allows you to easily reach the water and the victim. A second choice is to lay face down across the gunnels over the midthwart of your canoe. This position also allows you to easily reach the water and still maintain stability of your canoe. Your feet protrude from the opposite side to counterbalance your head and arms which are working over the victim's side of the canoe.

Administering artificial respiration on a victim in the water from the position lying across the gunnels of the canoe.

Artificial Respiration from the Canoe

The most important skill you may have to perform from your canoe is Artificial Respiration (AR) which must be initiated as soon as possible if there is to be any hope of a successful resuscitation of a non-breathing victim. To perform AR from the canoe on a victim still in the water, the rescuer assumes one of the two positions previously described. Roll the victim onto his back, alongside the canoe. Facing the victim, with the victim's head toward your right side, push your left arm between the victim's body and the victim's left arm. Continue to reach across, under the victim's back, until you can grasp the victim's upper right arm. This supports the victim's upper body. Your right hand can then come over the forehead, pinching the nose and tilting the head back.

If the victim does not resume spontaneous respirations after the initiation of artificial respiration, the artificial respiration will have to be continued during the entire rescue (see also Chapter 6, First Aid & Evacuation, page 113).

Dealing with the Panicking Victim

Capsizing may result in fear and anxiety which can lead to panic. Capsizing, can be a very disorienting event, especially in rough water conditions where a swimmer has severely limited vision. If the paddler was very far from shore when the capsize occurred, he may not be able to see the shoreline at all, and can rapidly lose all sense of direction. In rough conditions it is also very difficult for other canoeists to spot a capsized canoe and paddler. At this point the victim will realize that he is in very, if you will excuse the pun, deep trouble.

Cold water can also lead to panic. The water around where I live and paddle is very cold. The temperature of the rivers and lakes starts out at 2°C in the spring and rarely rises above 9°C all summer long. When you are plunged into water of this temperature you may find you can't breathe when your head comes out of the water. This isn't a psychological reaction, but a very physical response to the cold water. When the face, especially the forehead, hits freezing cold water, it initiates what we have left of the "mammalian diving reflex". This is a throwback from our evolutionary ancestors, when we used to have fins and flippers. The effect is to stop the breathing stimulus in your brain. This results in a very real sensation of tightness in the chest, breathlessness, and an inability to do anything but make weak gasping efforts to breath. While quite amusing to watch, it can cause real fear and panic in the swimmer.

Dealing with a panicking victim is a dangerous and risky problem at any time, but especially so when they are immersed in water. A panicking victim always creates a hazardous situation. Whether that hazard results in a problem almost always depends on the actions of the rescuers. Personally, in order to avoid trouble I never approach a panicky victim close enough to allow him to reach my canoe. I stay a good distance clear and throw the victim a flotation device of some kind. This might be an extra PFD, a packsack, or whatever is handy. Then it is a matter of talking to the victim and trying to get him to calm down and relax. Regardless of the location, lake or river, you should never let a panicking victim grab you or your canoe. If the victim remains panicky you simply have to wait him out. Eventually he will become too tired to be a danger, or you may even have to wait until he becomes unconscious. At that point you can deal with him with minimum danger to yourself.

The speed with which a panic situation can develop and magnify the problems became apparent to me a number of years ago while I was teaching a basic canoeing course. It was a beautiful summer day on a large, blue, mountain lake. We were having students capsize their canoes, very close to shore, and carry out some basic rescue skills. We always have the students capsize in a controlled situation early on in our programs, both to teach them the skills, but also to observe their reactions when they went into the water. Although the air was warm, a balmy 22°C, the lake was its usual 7-8°C. In this group we had two canoes, each with two instructors, and one canoe with two students, Steve and Bill. Steve was from the prairies and couldn't swim. However, he was wearing a good PFD, and had been comfortable in the water when we observed him in the pool. Bill could swim just fine. We are always very careful in our training programs because people's reactions are always unpredictable when they hit very cold water for the first time. Well, over went Steve and Bill, into the cold green water. Steve's face immediately burst above the surface, with eyes the size of dinner plates. He was in a total panic state. His eyes were staring off into space, and he was completely oblivious to any instructions or commands. He went into wild, uncontrollable, violent dog paddle motions with his arms and legs. At this point, he was floating quite well with the help of his PFD, and was in no immediate danger. However, four instructors were watching him intently from only a few feet away, and one was talking to him calmly and forcefully to try and reach his conscious mind. The problem was that while the instructors were focused on watching Steve, they were not paying very close attention to Bill. Bill had no water safety training at all, and his first instinct was to help out his friend Steve. Before anyone had a chance to stop him, Bill swam over and grabbed Steve's shoulder, in an attempt to help. However, Steve's brain and body were still on automatic. Before we knew it, Whack!, Bill got smacked directly in the eye by one of Steve's madly, violently thrashing elbows. Bill was knocked almost senseless. As his head went under, he tried to take a large breath of water and choked. At that moment we went from a hazardous but more or less controlled situation of one panicking victim, to a critical situation with two victims. One was panicking, and one was choking and about to panic. Our four instructors immediately went into action and both victims were easily assisted, and the situation defused. However, a similar situation happening where there were no skilled people ready to assist, could easily have ended in tragedy before anyone had a chance to intervene. Panicking victims are entirely unpredictable and extreme care must always be taken in dealing with them.

Assisting a Victim Back into his Canoe

Assisting a victim back into his own canoe can be managed in a couple of ways. One is to hold onto one gunnel of the victim's canoe while the victim climbs in from the opposite side. If you do this, it is important to tilt the canoe until the opposite gunnel is close to the water level, making it easier for the victim to climb in.

A second method is to bring the victim in between the ends of the two canoes. Facing the centre of the canoes, the victim then puts one hand on each deck or gunnel. Using both of the canoes for support, the victim can lift his legs up into the canoe.

Assisting a victim back into his own canoe.

Assisting the Victim into the Rescuer's Canoe

Performing AR, or providing any support to an injured victim in the water, is only a stop gap measure. Sooner or later you will have to try and get the victim into a canoe and then to shore. To do this by your self requires practice, and some physical strength. The best position for you is to be close to centre facing out from the canoe. Turn the victim so that his back is to the canoe, and reach under his right arm and across his chest with your right arm, until you can grasp his left wrist. Reach under his left arm with your left hand, across his chest, grasping his right wrist. You must then stand up and lift and pull the patient up across the gunnel into the canoe. This is a very unstable procedure when done by yourself, but it is a method that works.

If the victim has a canoe, it is easier to lift the victim into your canoe if you rescue his canoe first. Stabilize the victim as best you can, then perform a partial T-rescue on the capsized canoe. Begin the T-rescue as usual, lifting the end of the swamped canoe, and pulling it across until one third of the canoe is resting across yours, upside down over both gunnels. The overturned canoe, with the far end still in the water, acts like an outrigger, making your canoe effectively 5-6 metres wide instead of one metre wide. This forms a very stable working platform. In this position it is quite possible to safely stand up, walk around, even stand up on the gunnels with no fear of capsizing. Once you have created the platform, you will have a much easier and safer time lifting the victim into your canoe.

If you have a little more time available, another method of forming a stable platform, is to first perform a complete T-rescue on the victim's canoe. The empty canoe can then be brought alongside your canoe. In this position you can use a painter, or other rope, to quickly tie together the thwarts of both canoes. Once the thwarts are secured, the rescuer now has quite a stable platform from which to assist the victim.

If you have an assistant, the job becomes much easier. It works best if your assistant enters the water and stays on the opposite side of the canoe from the victim, holding onto the gunnel. This support allows the other rescuer to be more stable as he lifts out the victim.

Lifting a victim into your canoe, using a T-platform for stability.

Here the victim is able to assist by clenching her own hands together, so the rescuer is not using the crossed arms method used for helpless victims shown in the previous photo.

If the second canoe is available, a T-rescue platform is made as previously described. The assistant still provides the best help from in the water. This time the assistant holds onto the gunnel with one hand, and places the other hand underneath the thighs of the victim. With the assistant lifting at the same time as the rescuer in the canoe, the victim can easily be lifted into the canoe.

An assistant on the same side of the canoe, helping to lift a victim into the canoe.

Combining Rescue Techniques for more Efficient Rescues

Although towing, T-rescues, and throwbags, are distinct and separate techniques, they can all be combined to complete a rescue. If a T-rescue is in progress, it may be possible for a rescuer on shore with a throwbag to assist the rescuers on the water. Once the capsized canoe is across the rescue canoe, the shore rescuer can throw the throwbag to the rescue canoe and easily pull everyone to shore. Similarly, the throwbag can be used to assist in a towing rescue. If a rescuer on shore is in a suitable position, he can throw to the bowman of the rescue canoe and can again assist the rescuers by helping to pull everyone into shore.

A rescuer on shore may also be able to carry out a rescue much easier if he starts to assist before the crisis fully develops. This could be a situation where a canoe is becoming swamped in a set of rapids, to the point where maneuverability is limited and a capsize is very likely to happen before the paddlers can make it to shore. A rescuer can throw them a rope before their situation gets out of control with a capsize. The main consideration when throwing a rope to an upright canoe is not to pull them over, causing a capsize and making the situation that much worse. The rope should be thrown to the upstream person in the canoe. This person then holds the rope as close to the end of the canoe, and also as close to the surface of the water, as possible. As long as everyone is paying attention, this technique should allow the canoe to be pulled to shore without capsizing.

Z-drag in operation. Photo: Keith Morton

5

Rigging & Pulling Systems

More complex rescue situations can involve broached canoes, victims pinned in strainers, or victims trapped in positions with difficult access, and may require the use of many different skills and techniques to first gain access to the victim, and then safely rescue him.

The success of a rescue will depend on the ingenuity of the rescue leader. It is the rescue leader who must decide on the combination of rescue skills, methods of access, and techniques of rigging which will best utilize the available resources and result in the quickest, safest, and most efficient rescue.

Some Useful Knots for Rescue

Knots are very important for safety and rescue operations. Whenever you tie a knot, and especially during a rescue when you are under exceptional stress and pressure, there is always the chance of making a mistake. Unfortunately, a rescue is no time for anyone to be making a mistake, therefore, during a rescue you should tie as few knots as absolutely possible. If you use slings and carabiners, there should be few places where knots actually have to be tied.

Very few people work with ropes and rigging on a regular day to day basis. Many canoeists seem to suffer from a syndrome I call "knotophobia", an unreasoning fear of having to learn, tie and then depend on, knots. There appears to be a deep seated horror of forgetting which way the snake goes around the tree when he comes out of the hole.

If you are one of these people, then put your fears at rest. Knowing how to tie only two or three simple knots will allow you to carry out almost any rescue. Of course, the more knots you are familiar with, the more options you will have in an emergency.

A sling, carabiner, and figure eight knot.

Figure Eight

It is important that you learn to tie a loop at the end, or in the middle of a rope. Although there are a number of knots that will do this job, the easiest knot to learn and remember is the figure eight. Whenever you want to attach a rope to anything, a simple figure eight loop in the rope, plus a carabiner and a sling should do the job.

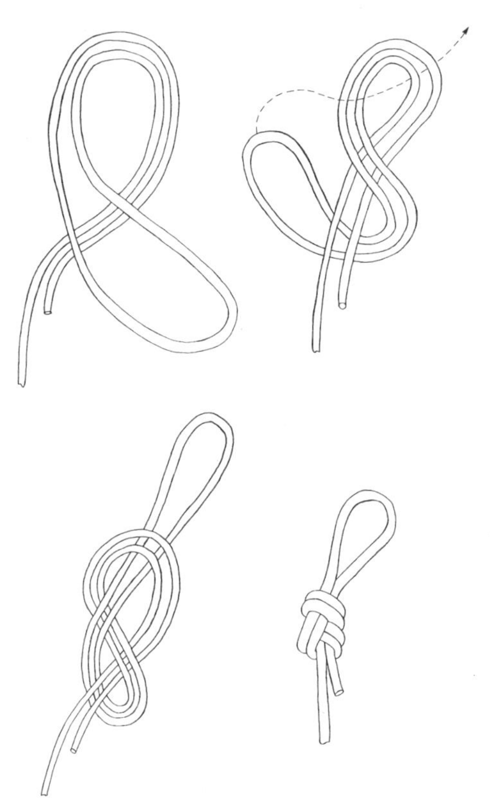

Tying a figure eight knot in the end or middle of a rope.

Clove Hitch

This knot is secure, simple to tie, easy to adjust or tighten, can be tied in the middle of the rope, and is easy to untie and release after it has been heavily loaded. It is used to fasten a rope, either at the end or in the middle, to a fixed anchor point such as a tree or post. Tied with a slipped, or incomplete loop, a clove hitch provides a very secure slip knot. Do not use a clove hitch if the object you are attaching it to is likely to rotate under load.

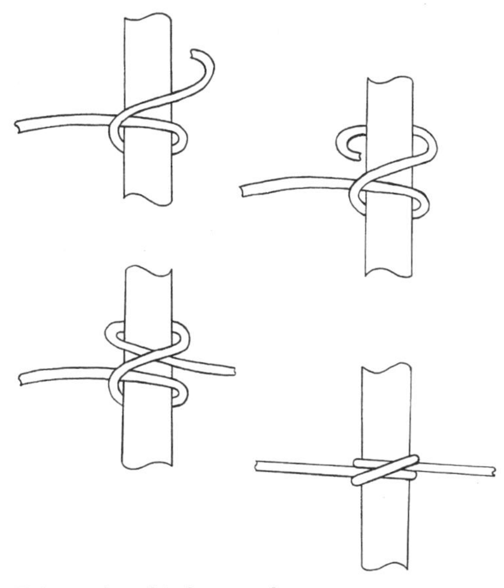

Tying a clove hitch around a post.

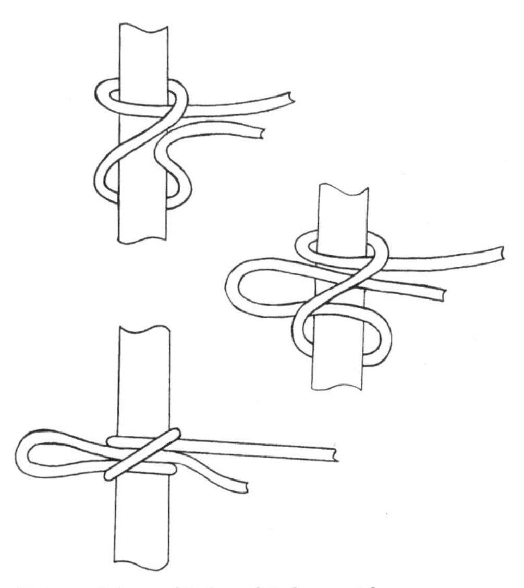

Tying a "slipped" clove hitch provides a secure knot which is easily released.

Prusik

A prusik knot provides a movable, secure, anchor point on another rope. In order to tie this knot, make a small sling, (prusik loop) from a piece of rope, not webbing, about 80 cm long. To function properly, use a rope at least one third less in diameter than the rope you will be tying it around. For example, a 6 mm prusik tied on a 9 mm rope. The prusik loop is applied to the main rope by passing the loop behind the rope and then threading the loop through itself twice. Once the loops are arranged so they do not cross each other, and then snugged up, the knot is secure. After this knot is tied, you can put your hand on it and slide it up and down the length of the rope. When you pull on the prusik loop itself, the knot locks, and provides a solid anchor point. If it slips, pass the loop through one more time.

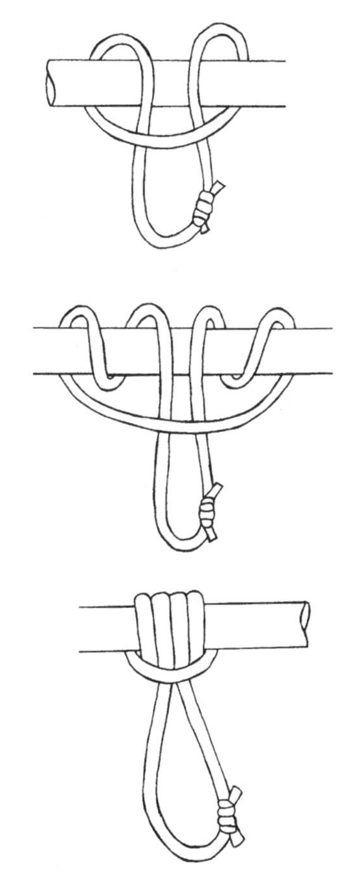

Tying a prusik knot around another, larger, rope.

The Fisherman's Knot

This is the knot used to tie two ends of rope together when you are making a sling or prusik loop. It is very secure and quite simple to tie. Since the Fisherman's knot is used to tie your slings before you go paddling, there should be no reason to have to try and remember how to tie this knot during a rescue.

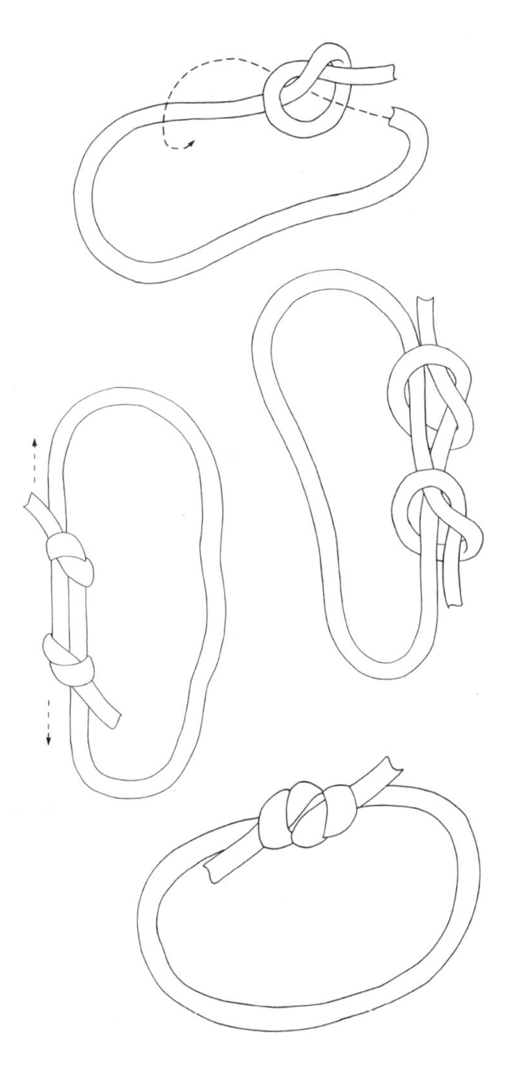

Tying a fisherman's knot in a loop of rope to make a sling.

Water Knot

The water knot, also known as the double overhand knot, is used to tie two ends of nylon webbing together. This is another knot that you can work on at home to make up slings.

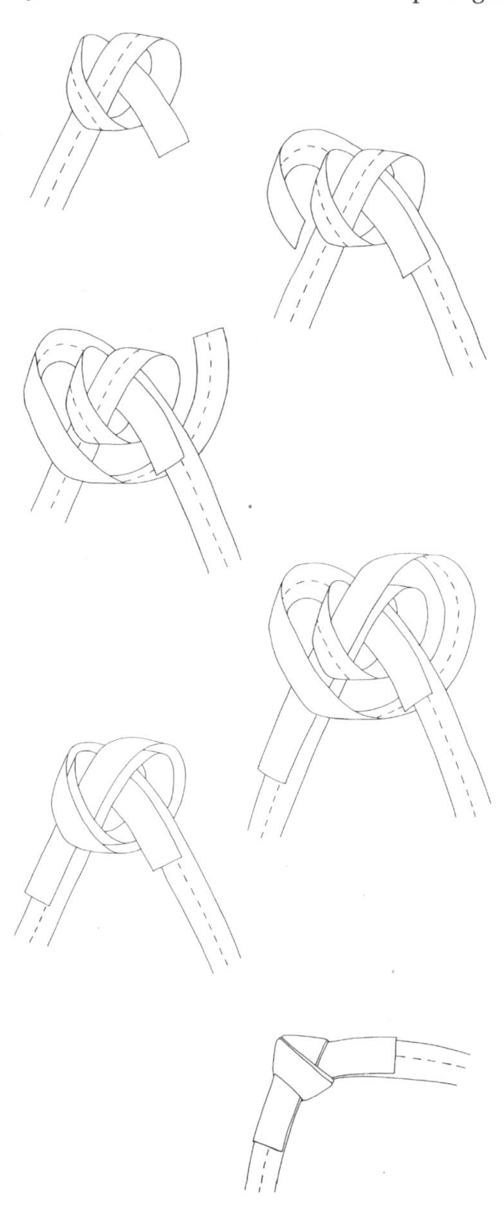

Tying two ends of nylon webbing together using a water knot.

Wrap Knot

If you need to tie a rope directly to an anchor point, and can't remember how to tie any of the knots, simply wrapping the rope a number of times around the anchor point and tucking in the loose end, will often do the job. As well as being quite secure, this tie can also be loosened while the rope is loaded.

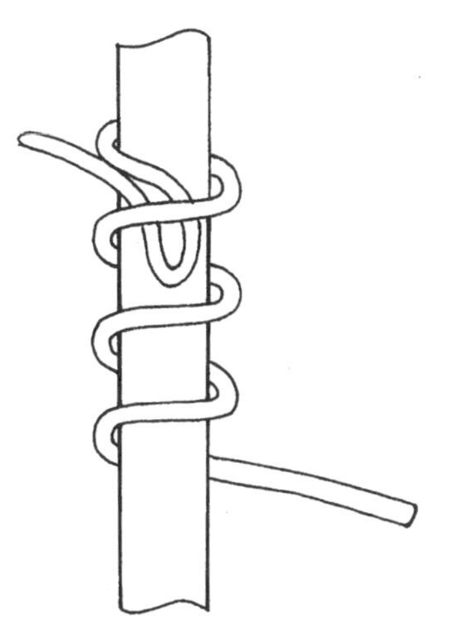

Making a wrap knot to secure the end of a rope.

The wrap knot used to attach the end of a rope to a tree.

Round Turn and Two Half Hitches

If you have to tie a rope directly to an anchor point such as a tree, this simple knot will provide security, and you can undo or loosen it while the rope is loaded.

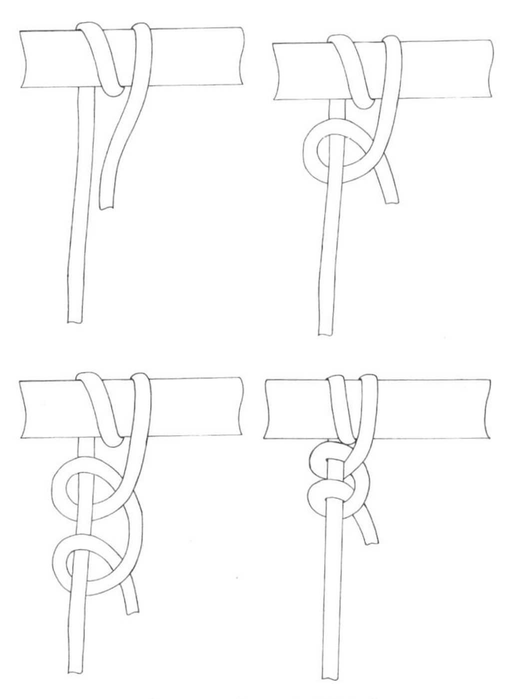

Tying a round turn and two half hitches.

These simple knots should be all you will need to actually tie during a rescue. All your slings and prusik loops should be tied and checked before you leave home. Just like all other technical skills, the rescue leader must be very careful about delegating individuals to tie knots and set ropes. You must be absolutely sure the person not only can tie the knot, but also understands the system you are trying to create.

How to Anchor a Rope

Anchoring a rope for a traverse line, or a pulling system, or for any other reason, can be a frustrating problem. Either the rope is too short to reach the anchor, or the anchor point is in the wrong place. Whenever I go to set up a rope there is never a tree in exactly the right spot, or there is a perfect spot on one side of the river, but not on the other. It can take some ingenuity to find a way to anchor the rope when no obvious anchor points can be found. When there are no suitable trees handy, either use a chockstone of some type, or use a "deadman" anchor.

A chockstone is something you tie the rope to, and then jam into a place which it cannot pull through. The chock can be a small rock, jammed in a converging crack between two large rocks, or a log or paddle, placed across a gap between two rocks with the rope attached to its centre.

A branch or paddle can be used as a chock to attach a rope.

A log or paddle buried in the ground makes a very secure deadman anchor. Depth of burial required will depend upon the firmness of the gravel and on the angle of pull.

A log buried under a pile of rocks makes a very secure deadman anchor. This photo shows the early stages of securing the deadman. In practice, a large pile of rocks is needed.

Constructing a deadman anchor involves tying the rope to an object, then burying the object as firmly as possible in the ground. The most secure type of a deadman anchor is a log, a metre or so long, with the rope tied to the centre of it. The log is then buried in ground at 90° to the angle of pull. If you can't dig in the ground, a log such as this can be buried by piling rocks on top of it. If logs are unavailable, the rope can be tied to a good sized rock, and the rock can be buried in the ground, or under a pile of other rocks. Whatever method is used, the rope to the deadman must enter the ground at as low an angle as possible so that there is a minimum tendency to pull the deadman upward out of the ground.

It may be necessary to set up a rope across a river, well above the level of the water. One way to solve this problem where there are no large trees, is to use two small trees in line as an anchor. The rope is tied around the first tree with a clove hitch at the required height. The tail of the rope is then tensioned as much as possible and tied to the base of the second tree. This anchors the rope and prevents the first tree from bending under the load.

A similar system can be made with an A-frame constructed from logs, saplings, or paddles. The logs to form the A-frame are tied together at the top using a clove hitch. Once the rope is secured to the top of the A-frame, the tail of the rope is tied down to an anchor behind. The height of the rope can be adjusted by opening or closing the frame at the base of the "A".

A-frames provide excellent vertical support, but they may become quite unstable if there is any significant sideways pull. This problem can be lessened by keeping the base of the "A" as wide as possible. You can also bury the ends of the legs of the A-frame a few centimetres into the ground, or pile some heavy rocks around the bottom of the legs of the A-frame to help stabilize it.

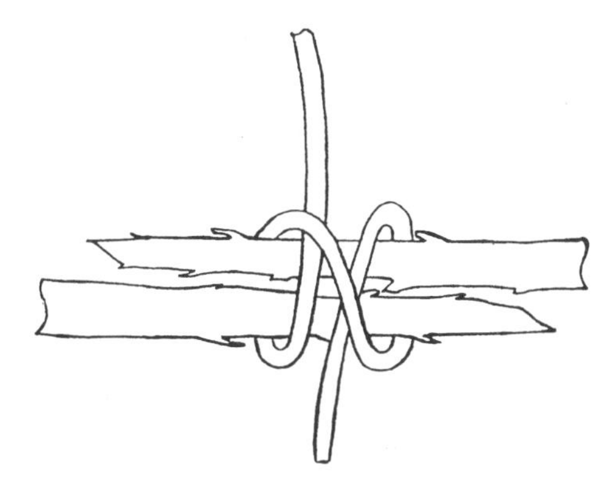

The top of an A-frame is tied together with a clove hitch.

An A-frame can be used to support a rope above the surface of the river.

Rigging a Rope Across a River

The way you choose to transport a rope across a river depend on the width of the river, and on the resources that you have available.

If the river is narrow enough, you may be able to throw a single throwbag across. If the river is wider, two throwbags can be used as follows. One rescuer wades or is ferried to the middle, and then throws a throwbag to each shore.

When taking a rope across a river, you first start with the lightest, smallest diameter line that you have. This becomes a "tag line" (a line across a river manipulated by a person on each side), and is used to pull across your main rope.

To walk a rope across the river, use any of the previously mentioned foot crossing methods. It is important is to keep the rope out of the water to prevent unneccessary drag due to the force of the current. The rope can be carried by hand, or by a large loop passed over the head and one shoulder.

If you have to swim the rope across do so where there are as few obstacles as possible to minimize the chances of entanglement. Swimming a rope is best done with a large loop passed over the head and one shoulder. Any kind of long line in the current produces tremendous amounts of drag. You must be prepared for significant downstream travel. If there is someone on the far side, have them throw a throwbag to the swimmer to assist him ashore.

Ferrying a line across a river with a canoe may be the quickest method. Ideally, it is done with three people in the canoe. One person, on their knees in the centre of the canoe, holds the end of the line above his head. The paddlers then execute a forward ferry across the river. It is more difficult to ferry a line if only two paddlers are available. In this case, the bow person carries the line, loosely in one hand. It is important that both the rescuer in the canoe, and the rescuers on shore, carefully control the tension on the rope. If it dips into the current, it can be ripped out of the canoe carriers hands, or cause the canoe to capsize.

Using a Rope Across a River

Once a traverse rope is stretched across a river it is called a **traverse rope** and it can be used for more purposes than just a handhold for rescuers. To be of use in most rescue situations, the traverse rope must be as taut as possible at all times. This means that a tensioning system should be in place to make the rope tight, and to maintain the tension as the rope stretches and sags as it is loaded and when it gets wet. The easiest way to develop a tensioning system for a traverse rope is to use the 3:1 pulley system (Z-drag) described on page 100-101.

Tag Lines

A tag line is a rope across the river which is managed from both sides by people holding on to it. A tag line is usually two throwbag ropes connected by a carabiner, or a single rope with a loop and carabiner in the centre.

A tag line made from two ropes joined by a carabiner.

Once the tensioning is complete, the traverse rope must be tied to the anchor independently of the Z-drag. In any rescue, a tag line should always be kept at the ready, independent of other systems you may have in place. With a handler on each side of the river, the centre of the tag line can be moved back and forth, and upstream or downstream, to any position on the river.

A tag line can be used to transport equipment or people to the accident site, or across the river. Light equipment or a main rescue rope can be attached directly to the centre of the tag, and the rescuers simply keep tension on the line as they pull the equipment across. In narrow rivers, or reasonably moderate currents, a canoe can be attached to the centre of the tag line and moved back and forth by the rope handlers on shore to move equipment or people. However, if the current is strong, more support for the canoe will be needed than can be provided by a single tag line.

A tag line can also function as an immediate stabilization line for a trapped victim. Victims who are pinned or trapped partially underwater, or who are in some deteriorating situation, may be able to hold themselves in a more stable position if a tag line can be conveyed to them immediately to provide a firm handhold.

Lines such as this can also be used to release victims from entrapment situations. When a victim is pinned in a river, whether against a strainer, or with their foot trapped between two rocks, the only way to free them is to pull them directly upstream against the current, exactly opposite to the direction that they went in. Set a tag line downstream of the pinned victim. The centre of the line is then weighted, possibly with the throwbag full of rocks. The weight is then moved to a position just downstream of the trapped victim. The weight is allowed to take the line underwater. The rescuers can then pull directly upstream, hopefully catching the pinned victim and pulling him upstream against the current, freeing him from the entrapment. In this situation, the longer the tag line is, the more the rescuers will be able to pull directly upstream, increasing the efficiency of the rescue.

A tag line used to pull a larger rope across a river.

A canoe attached directly to the centre of a tag line can be used to move people or equipment across a river.

Controlling a Working Platform for On-Water Rescue

To work safely at an accident site in the middle of a river, or to transport equipment back and forth across a river safely, requires some type of working platform. To reach an accident site in moderate currents, a single canoe can be used as a working platform. To provide support and allow control of the platform, a tensioned traverse rope is used. Attach the canoe directly to a traverse rope by means of a carabiner and a sling fastened to the bow or stern seat. The carabiner can slide along the rope as a rescuer in the canoe moves the canoe across the current by pulling hand over hand on the traverse line. If the canoe is attached by an end loop or fixed point at the very end of the canoe, or if there is not going to be a rescuer in the canoe, it will be difficult to reach the rope to move the canoe. To make the system completely independent of any person in the canoe, the centre of a tag line can be fastened directly to the upstream end of the canoe. The movement of the canoe is then completely controlled by the rope handlers on shore. A river crossing system like this can be used to transport people across the river, even if they have no great level of canoeing expertise themselves.

A canoe attached directly to a traverse line, with lateral movement controlled by a tag line. See the top diagram on the page opposite.

A working platform in use. Photo: Keith Morton.

A traverse line system can be used to get a canoe directly to the accident site. It may be possible to anchor the traverse rope in position just upstream of the site so that the canoe, under control of the rope handlers, can be moved directly to the victim. In many cases however, it will not be possible to anchor your traverse rope at exactly the right spot to allow direct access of the platform to the victim. You will have to rig the platform to move independently downstream of the traverse rope by attaching a rope to the upstream end of the platform, running it through a carabiner attached to a sling on the traverse rope, and back down to the platform. The rescuer in the platform can now lower the platform downstream from the traverse rope by paying out the rope between the canoe and the traverse rope. Alternatively, the rope from the platform could go through the carabiner in the sling and to a controller on shore, and the shore handler can move the platform down and up to the traverse rope. While this system may sound complicated, it is just a combination of a number of simple components. A system such as this can allow you to precisely place your working platform anywhere on the river.

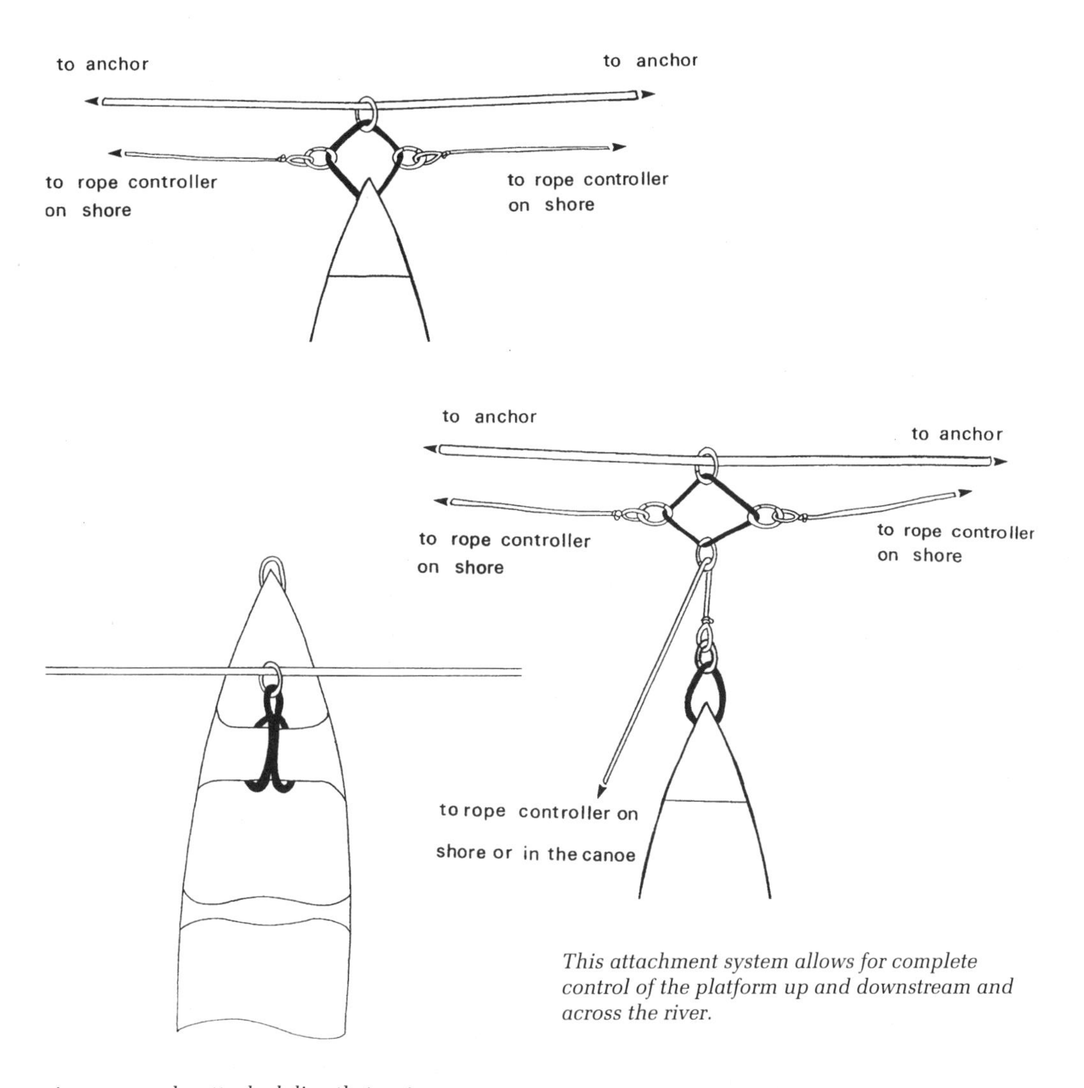

This attachment system allows for complete control of the platform up and downstream and across the river.

A canoe can be attached directly to a traverse rope to form a working platform.

In rough water a single canoe may not provide sufficient stability or safety. You can make a more stable working platform by tying two canoes together to form a raft. Cut two saplings and lash them securely across the bow and stern seats of the two canoes. Make sure that the centre lines of the canoes are parallel when the platform is complete. This makes it easier to control in rough water. This type of platform is very stable, allowing 2-3 rescuers easy and safe movement while they are working. While allowing access to the accident site, a platform such as described here may also be used to transport an injured victim across the river. When the platform is complete it is attached to the traverse line as previously described.

A canoe platform needs to be carefully controlled. Whether it is made by using one canoe or two canoes, the platform will still want to surf on waves and make eddy turns as you move it across the current. Control of the platform itself can be by two methods. You can have a paddler or two in the platform to steer and control the downstream end. Another method is to use a second tag line. A second tag line at the downstream end of the platform, managed by two more rope handlers provides a four line system which can allow precise control of the platform.

A full lowering system such as this is rarely necessary in a rescue. When you deal with any kind of technical rescue on a river, always strive to keep your systems as simple as possible. The more complicated the system is, the longer it takes to set up, and the greater the chance of mistakes being made, which increases the risk to the rescuers and to the victim.

Use painters to quickly lash the thwarts of two canoes side by side to form a temporary platform.

A double canoe platform attached to a traverse rope.

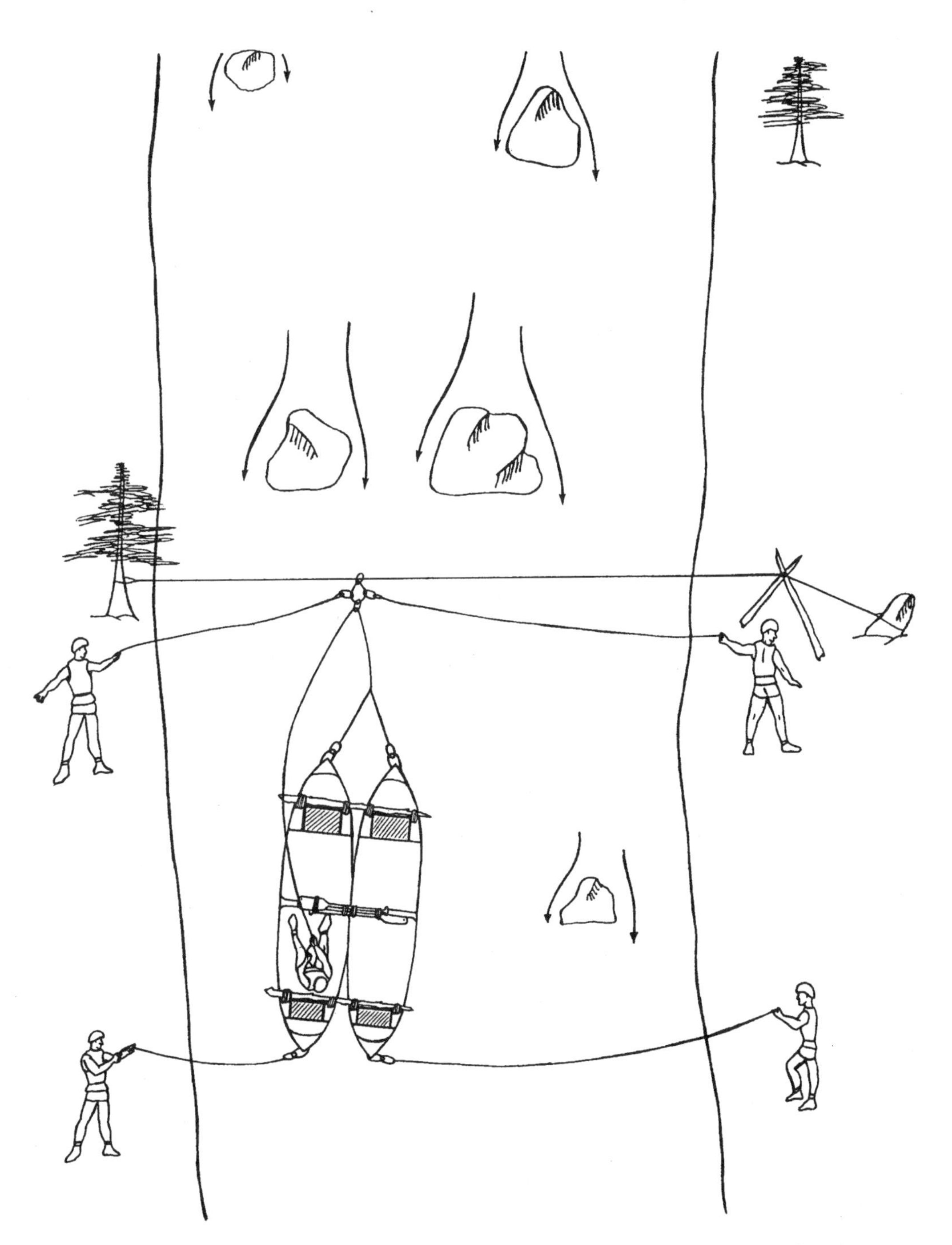

A four line control system for a double canoe platform. The people at the downstream end can be dispensed with if the raft is manned with paddlers who can steer. However, having the downstream controllers on shore provides much more space in the platform for the rescuers to work. The downstream lines allow the platform to be securely tied in place once it is in position.

How to Set up Useful Pulling Systems

You often end up needing to pull something during a rescue operation. The ability to utilize and combine different types of pulling systems is a useful skill for a rescuer to acquire. For example, you may need to pull a broached canoe off a rock, dismantle a logjam, hoist three weeks food into a tree away from bears, tension a traverse line, or clear fallen trees off a remote river access logging road.

The quickest way to move anything is to get as many people as possible on a rope, and pull. Used in conjunction with other techniques, this should be a prime resource in your repertoire of skills.

Using the Force of the River by Building a "Sea-Anchor"

The other resource that you have ready at hand is the force of the river itself. Make the river work for you by creating a device which you can use as a sea-anchor in the current. Anything that has a large surface area and just barely floats will produce an enormous force when attached to a rope and placed in the current. A bucket or two will work. A capsized canoe makes an excellent sea-anchor, and a bundle of logs will work well. The advantage of a bundle of logs is that it can be discarded, and you can add a few at a time to gradually increase the pull.

A sea-anchor provides a powerful force directly in line with the current. The amount of force you get depends on the size of the sea anchor and the speed of the current. Because you can't switch off the current, it is almost impossible to stop the pulling of a sea-anchor once it is in place, and you must be prepared to cut it loose. If the sea-anchor is made from something that you want to keep, such as a canoe, buckets, or packs, you must be ready with a plan of action for its retrieval. See page 107.

Using pure manpower to retrieve a pinned canoe.

Using Angle Pulls

You can create a large increase in the force at the end of a taut rope by pulling at right angles in the middle of the rope. Secure one end of the rope to a solid anchor point, and fasten the other end to the load. Tighten the rope as much as possible. By pulling at right angles to the main rope, you can deliver a multiplied inward force at the ends of the main rope. The amount of force that you can develop depends on how much the anchor rope can be tightened and kept straight. If the rope can be kept absolutely straight, the pulling force is very powerful.

The amount of force developed with this method drops off dramatically as the main rope deviates from absolutely straight, or 180°. When the angle reaches 160°, the inward force at the ends of the rope is three times the pulling force that you are applying in the centre of the rope, and at 120° the forces are exactly equal with no advantage at all. Below 120°, you are actually getting less force delivered to your load when you use this method. Although often proposed as a handy way to get some increased force in your systems, angle pulls are not very practical. It is very difficult to keep any length of rope, especially long spans of wet nylon rope, tightened to straighter than 160°. This means that the actual amount of advantage that you get using this method is rarely going to be worth the trouble of setting it up. It is usually much more efficient to use a pulley system.

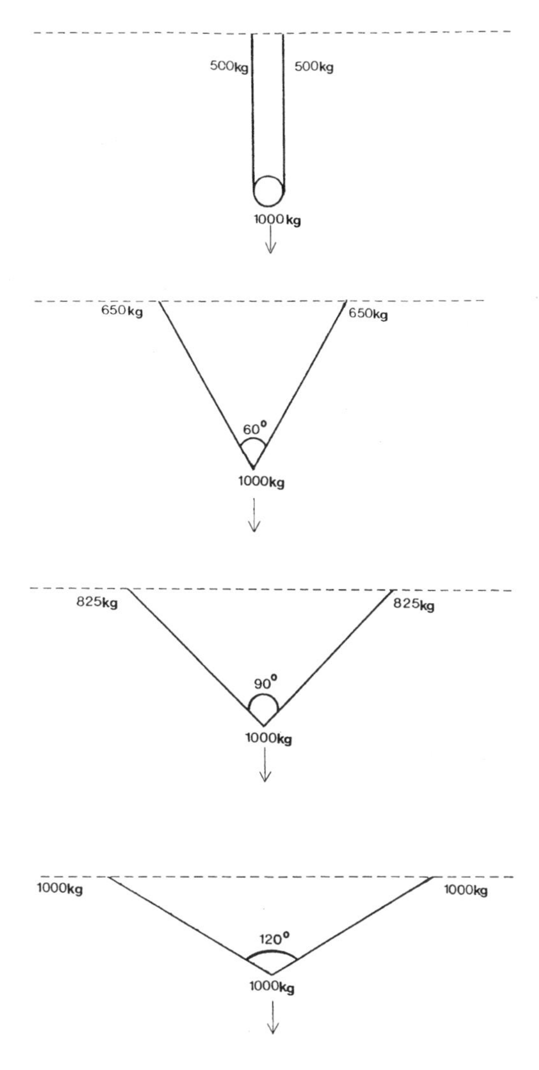

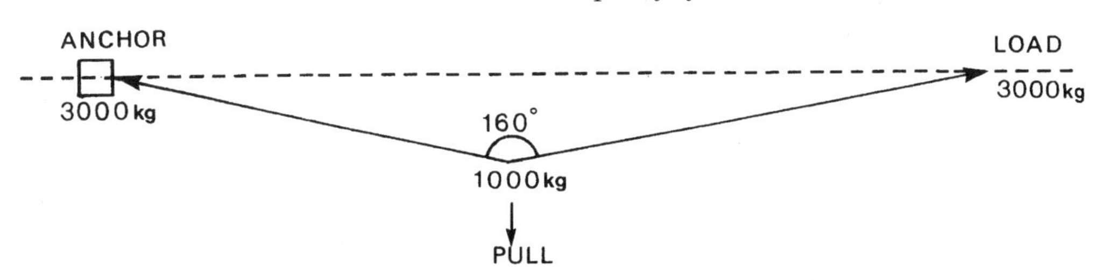

Angle pulls can be used to increase the force of your pulling system, however they are usually limited in application as the increased force rapidly drops off as the angle of pull increases.

Simple but Powerful Pulley Systems

Ropes and carabiners can be used to set up simple pulley systems to increase the power of pull or provide "increased mechanical advantage". Pulley systems are not complicated, and by learning only one or two basic systems, you can combine them any number of ways to increase the mechanical advantage of the entire system.

An easy way to determine the amount of the mechanical advantage is to measure the amount of rope you pull in, and compare it to how far the load moves. For example, if you pull in two metres of rope, and the load moves one metre, you have a 2:1 mechanical advantage. This is the system shown below. Here a pulley is located on the load. In order to raise a 50 kg weight by one metre, you must pull with a force of 25 kg for a distance of two metres.

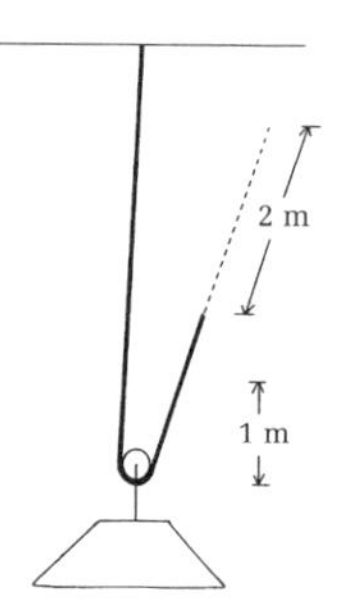

A pulley system which provides 2:1 mechanical advantage.

Compare the diagram above with the system shown below. This is 1:1 system with no mechanical advantage. The pulley is not mounted on the load, and it provides no increase in the mechanical advantage, it only changes the direction of your pull. To raise the load by one metre, you have to pull in one metre of rope, so it is a 1:1 system.

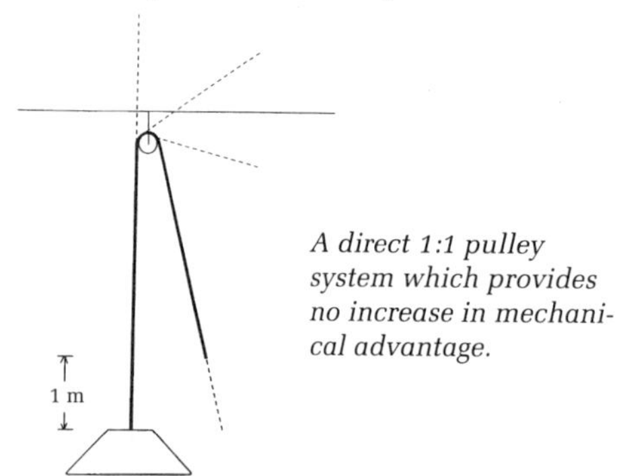

A direct 1:1 pulley system which provides no increase in mechanical advantage.

There are two different ways to combine pulleys. You can combine them in a parallel fashion, where the mechanical advantage of each system is added together, or you can combine them in series (in line), where the mechanical advantage of each system is multiplied together. Because we want to generate the most mechanical advantage for a given pull, we will look at both methods of combining systems.

The most commonly used pulley set up is a 3:1 system, sometimes called the "Z-drag", which can be constructed in the field with the minimum of materials. The simplest way to construct a 3:1 system is to combine the 1:1 pulley and the 2:1 pulleys. In order to raise the load by one metre, you must pull in 3 metres of rope. Using this system you can raise a 90 kg load one metre, by pulling with a force of 30 kg for a distance of 3 metres.

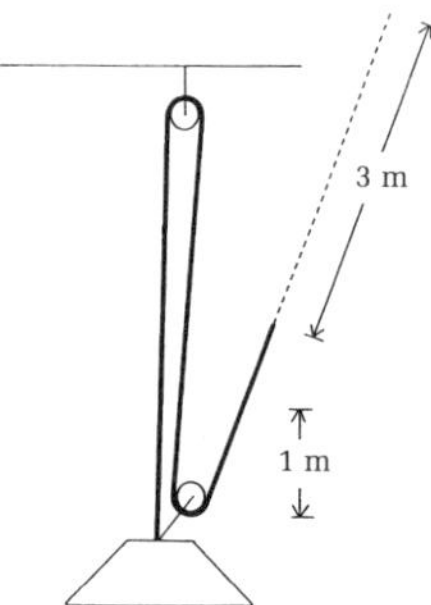

The commonly used 3:1 pulley system is created by combining a 2:1 and 1:1 system.

All you need to construct this system is a rope, a couple of carabiners and a couple of prusiks. Fix one end of the rope to the load. Run the rope through a carabiner at your anchor point to a second carabiner attached to the load. By pulling in the direction of the anchor, you can now apply a 3:1 mechanical advantage to the load; the carabiners function as pulleys allowing free travel of the rope. The carabiners can be replaced with specialized rescue pulleys which reduce the amount of friction in the system, providing smoother operation and easier pulling.

If the load is too far away to allow the second pulley carabiner to be attached directly to the load, it can be fixed to the main rope by means of a prusik loop. If you need to move a load a long distance, or you have a short pulling range, you need to apply a locking device to hold the load while you re-advance the pulley on the prusik, for the next pull. This is done by tying a second prusik loop to the rope leading to the load, and then attaching the loop to the carabiner at your anchor point. While you pull on the drawing rope, the rope to the load slides through this "brake" prusik. Because this prusik tends to jam against the carabiner you must constantly monitor it. When your first prusik has been drawn all the way to the anchor, you can release the tension and the "brake" prusik automatically locks and holds the load. You can then slide the first prusik back towards the load and repeat the process. This is the system shown in the three diagrams below.

A 3:1 pulley system using one rescue pulley to provide smoother pulling in a Z-drag.

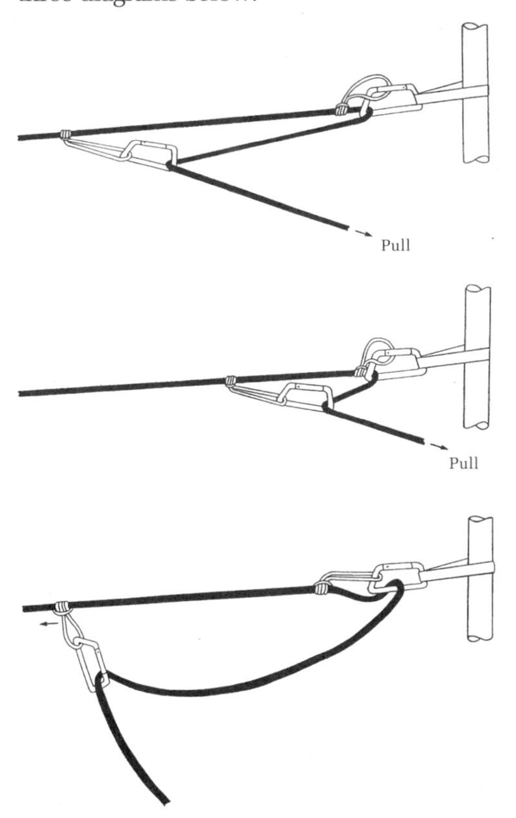

A 3:1 pulley system, or "Z-drag", using carabiner and prusik loops.

The most efficient 3:1 pulley system uses two rescue pulleys to minimize friction.

You can create a very simple 3:1 pulley system with nothing more than a single piece of rope by attaching the rope to the load and passing it around the anchor point. Pass the free end through a slip knot tied in the rope from the load. If you have no carabiners at all this can allow you to create some mechanical advantage. Also known as the Trucker's hitch, or Packer's hitch, this method does develop quite a bit of friction depending on the type of rope, and roughness of the anchoring point.

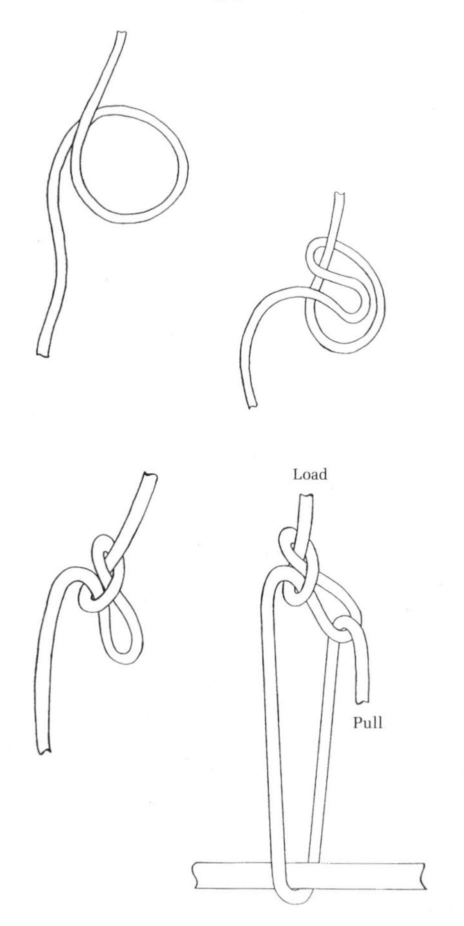

A simple 3:1 system using only a single piece of rope.

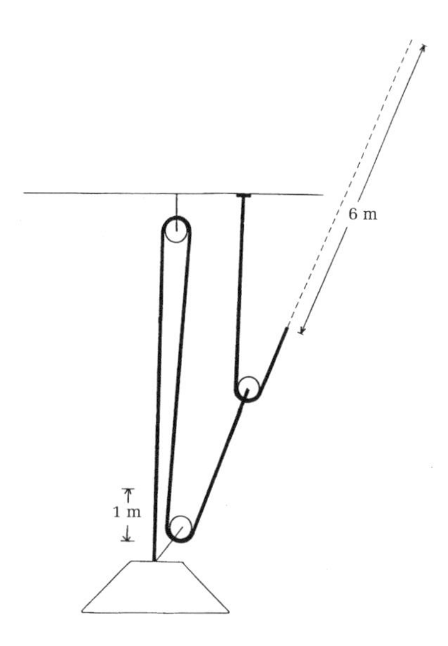

A 6:1 pulley system created by combining a 3:1 system and a 2:1 system.

You can add another pulley in series with the 3:1 system in order to increase the mechanical advantage. The diagram above shows a standard 3:1 pulley, with a 2:1 pulley system applied to the end of the drawing rope. This produces a 6:1 mechanical advantage. In order to move load 1 one metre, 3 metres must be pulled through the 3:1 system. To pull the second system by three metres, you must pull six metres through the 2:1 system.

Theoretically, by continuing to combine these basic systems you can increase the mechanical advantage indefinitely. Unfortunately, friction soon becomes the limiting factor even if you can replace all the carabiners with pulleys. Pulleys are lots of fun to play with. You can experiment with models using paper clips and string to determine the mechanical advantage for various systems.

Systems for Lowering and Delivering Rope in a Controlled Manner

It is always worth while to have some sort of system available for lowering people and equipment by means of a rope. It is not uncommon to be faced with steep river banks, or canyon walls, where you may need to lower people or equipment to assist a victim or access an accident scene. Lowering systems are also very useful if you are evacuating a patient on a stretcher over rough terrain, but always be particularly aware of the possibility of you or the rope dislodging rocks or other debris onto those below.

Dealing with very steep terrain demands skill, equipment, and experience. Extra care must be taken to ensure the continuous safety of the rescuer and the victims. Performing technical, free swinging, vertical lowering off bridges or cliffs is **potentially very dangerous** and should be avoided unless you have specialized training and equipment.

Never use polypropylene rope for lowering operations, either as the main rope or as a backup. Polypropylene rope has poor resistance to shock loading, may be severely weakened by the heat of friction around carabiners and has unreliable strength after use and exposure to sunlight.

Using the Body Belay

A simple body belay can be set up rapidly and easily, but is the least safe and most difficult system to control for inexperienced users. To perform a body belay, sit with your legs out, preferably with feet braced solidly against a rock or log in front of you. It is highly advisable for you to be securely tied in to a solid anchor point whenever possible. If no anchor sling is available, the end of the lowering rope can be used to tie you in, although ideally, the tying-in system should be totally independent of the lowering system.

Pass the rope from the load, through your guiding hand, around and across your back above the anchor rope, and out through the controlling hand.

The friction necessary to control the lower is created by the rope passing through your hands and around your body. The friction can be increased by bringing the control hand across the front of your body, thus increasing the contact area between the rope and the belayer. At no time should you ever wrap the rope around your wrists or arms; in the event of a sudden jerk on the rope the wraps will reduce your control and possibly put you in danger. To perform a sitting belay properly you should be equipped with gloves and a thick jacket or PFD to prevent rope burn and abrasion injuries.

An easier and safer alternative to a body belay is to use a carabiner as a friction device for a lowering system. However, you will require a sling and an anchor point. Two simple ways to do this are using a friction wrap or a friction hitch.

Using a body belay to lower equipment down a steep slope.

Using the Carabiner Friction Wrap

A friction wrap is achieved by wrapping the lowering rope two or three times around the long side of the carabiner. The number of wraps depends on the diameter of the lowering rope, and the weight of the load that you are lowering. This is probably the easiest system to remember, and the least likely to be done incorrectly. If in doubt, put more turns on than you think you will need, and take one off if there is too much friction.

Wrapping the lowering rope around the long axis of a carabiner provides a simple friction control for lowering.

Using the Carabiner Friction Hitch

If you can remember how to tie it properly, you can use a friction hitch, also known as a "Munter Hitch", which is a type of knot, tied directly to the carabiner.

The advantage to friction wraps, and friction hitches, is that even if you should let go of the rope completely, there should still be enough friction in the system to prevent a rapid fall. Another advantage is that they keep you as independent from the system as possible. This means that if things go badly wrong you are less likely to be pulled into the river or down a cliff.

A successful lowering system depends on having a secure anchor point, a properly functioning lowering device, and a dependable lowering rope. If you do not have **all three** of these components, you should never be trying to lower a victim or a rescuer. Remember, the guiding principle is not to make the situation any worse, so you should not perform techniques which put the rescuers at risk.

The friction (Munter) hitch is a knot which provides excellent control for a lowering system. If you wish to take in slack, the knot inverts and allows you to pull the rope in.

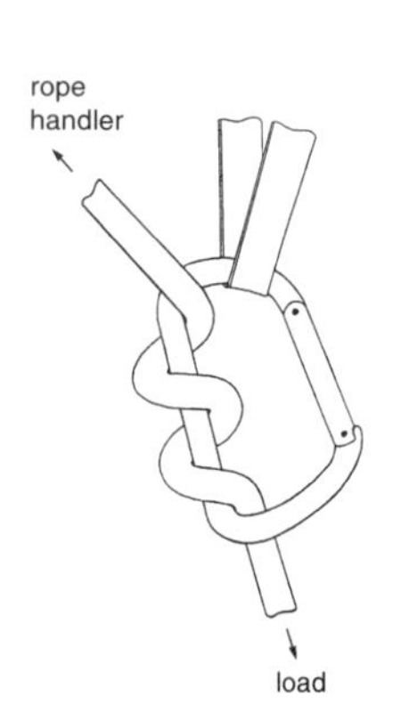

Friction Wrap

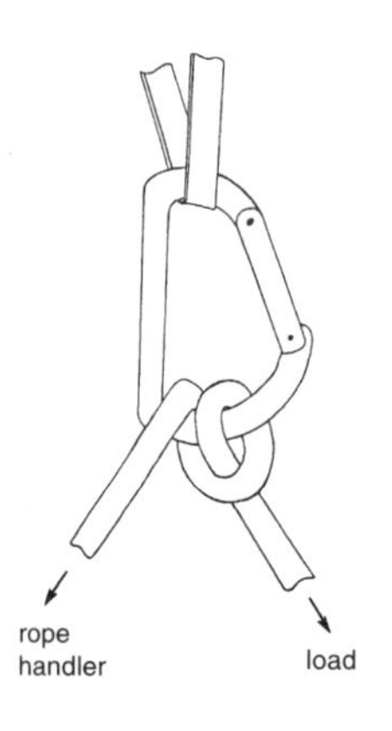

Friction (Munter) Hitch

Attaching the Rescuer to the End of a Lowering Rope

The most comfortable way (for the person being lowered) to tie into the end of a rope is to use a sling and a locking carabiner. The sling should be a little longer than usual, about the distance from the point of your shoulder to the end of your opposite arm. Wear the sling diaper fashion, with two loops coming around the waist, and the third loop pulled up between the legs. These three loops are all connected by a carabiner, and snapped into a small loop at the end of the lowering rope. Remember, this is for operations on dry land, **never** in moving water!

Lowering or raising people and equipment on steep terrain is quite dangerous, particularly since the footwear worn by many paddlers in not suited to clambering on steep or rough terrain. Whenever possible, a separate safety line should always be attached to the person being lowered and should be belayed completely independently from the main system.

A sling worn "diaper fashion" provides an easily-constructed harness to connect someone to the end of a rope.

Techniques for Recovering Pinned or Broached Canoes

Open canoes have a habit of becoming pinned or broached against rocks, bridge abutments, or any other obstacle that happens to be in a river. Recovering broached canoes can be a difficult problem and there are many ways to approach the situation depending on how many people are available and what resources you have.

Retrieval of a canoe must be done with care. It carries all the same hazards and dangers as any other rescue, and can generate additional high risks, for possibly a very limited benefit. Because of the unfavourable risk/benefit ratio of this activity, a canoe or equipment recovery should never be carried out in the risky, high-speed "rescue mode". However, if you are on a remote wilderness trip, where the loss of equipment could be a major factor in your future survival, it may be understandable to accept a slightly higher risk in order to recover your equipment.

When you are retrieving a broached canoe you must keep in mind what will happen when it comes free of the pinned position. You do not want to injure yourself, and you do not want to lose the equipment again, or lose more equipment. A line should always be attached to the canoe, to control it after it comes free. Always attempt to avoid working immediately downstream of any pinned object. A canoe may behave in a completely unpredictable manner when it comes free and could cause serious injury to anyone who may be in the way.

When a canoe becomes pinned, it is essential to initiate the recovery as quickly as possible without getting into the risky rescue mode. This is because the longer you delay, the more difficult retrieval may become. Depending on the speed of the current, and the amount of the canoe that is underwater, the canoe may not initially deform a great deal. However, the longer the current works on the canoe, the more it will be deformed, and the deeper it may be pushed underwater, making recovery increasingly difficult.

Using a pendulum traverse to gain access to a broached canoe. Retrieval should be initiated as soon as possible, before the canoe becomes severely deformed by the force of the current.

Eddy Lift

Pinned canoes are held in place by the force of the current. The pressure of the water forcing the canoe against the obstacle creates friction, preventing the canoe from being slid free. This is one situation where you somehow have to work against the power of the current.

A quick method of recovering a pinned canoe is known as the "Eddy Lift". The idea behind this technique is to deflect the force of the current, allowing the canoe to be freed from the obstacle. This method requires reasonably shallow water. Five to six people wade into the current just upstream of the pinned canoe. Forming a tight group, and squatting down in the current, the mass of people forms an obstacle in the river, creating an eddy of still water around the pinned canoe. The canoe can then be lifted quickly and easily off the obstacle. I once used this technique in a small canyon to recover, in a matter of minutes, a canoe which had been completely wrapped around a boulder.

If the water is a little too fast for the people to remain in position, a rope can be used to assist the procedure. As in a pendulum river crossing, the rope is attached as far upstream as possible, and the group holds onto the downstream end. They can now wade out and perform the maneuver in faster water with less chance of being pushed off their feet. However this method should not be used if the rescuers are at risk of becoming pinned or entrapped in the same feature which is holding the canoe.

If you have a suitable supply of rocks upstream of the canoe, and plenty of time on your hands, it may be possible to build a "cofferdam" with rocks and logs to deflect the force of the current.

If you can't deflect the current, you need to pull and manhandle the canoe off the obstacle, against the full force of the current. It may be near impossible to pull a canoe directly upstream against a strong current; you have to lift the canoe up and over the obstruction, or slide it off to one side.

Sea Anchor Pull

One method is to use a sea anchor to put the power of the river to work for you. The best place to attach the sea anchor is on the very end of the canoe that you are trying to lift or pull off. By using a sea anchor on the long end of the pinned canoe, you can create a great deal of additional force which helps you to lever the canoe off the obstruction as you lift, lever, pry, and pull on the other end.

The important consideration in this technique is to first have the broached canoe tethered to maintain control once it comes free. You must also keep in mind that sea anchors will continue to pull once the canoe is free. You should have a release system for the sea anchor in place, or a knife handy to cut it free.

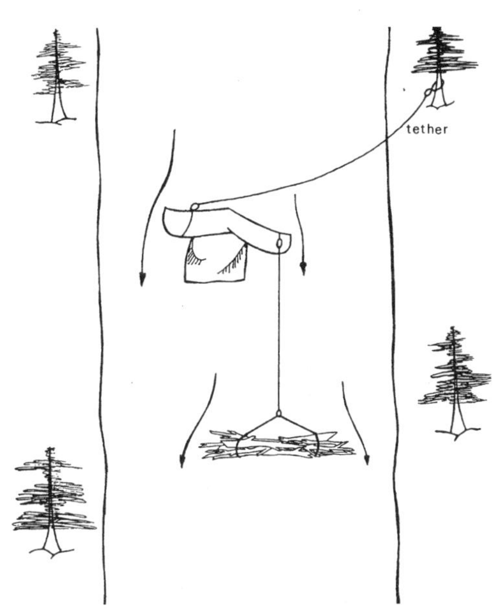

Using a bundle of logs as a sea anchor to grab the current and pull the canoe free. Once it is free, you must be able to release the sea anchor.

Rope Pull Systems

Another option is to use a rope pull system to allow you to pull the canoe clear of the obstruction. A 3:1 or 6:1 pulley system with a few people pulling on it should allow you to pull a canoe out of most situations.

Attaching a rope properly to the pinned canoe is important to a successful recovery. Individual attachment points such as thwarts and seats are, if used on their own, insufficient to withstand a powerful pulling system. A rope can be attached to a seat or to a thwart if it then passes around the body of the canoe to distribute the force as much as possible. Passing the rope around the canoe also helps in the recovery of the canoe because it imparts a rolling force to the canoe. Whether you pass the rope over or under the canoe depends on how the canoe is pinned and therefore which way you want it to roll. If the canoe is pinned with the high side tilted upstream, the rope is

To pull a broached canoe, the rope can be attached to a canoe using a sling and carabiner.

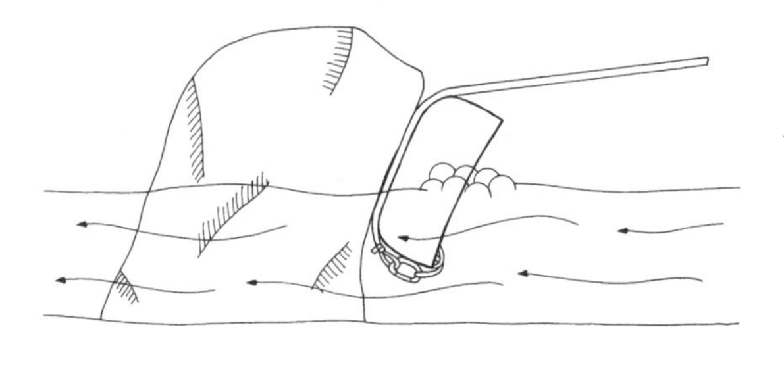

When the high side of the canoe is tilted upstream and is well above water, attach the rope so that it passes over the canoe to your pulling point.

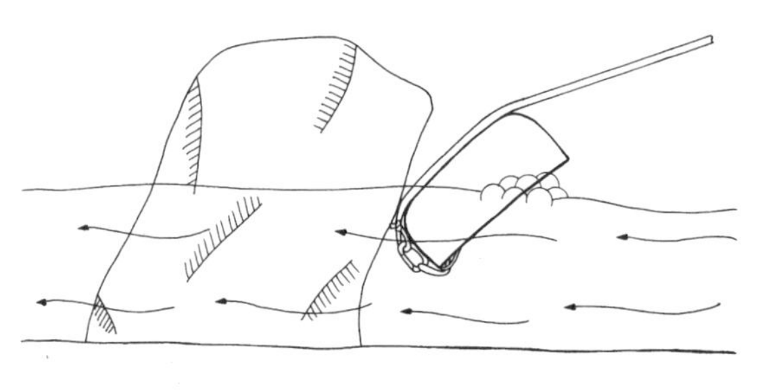

As you pull, the canoe is rolled away from the obstacle, clearing it from the pin.

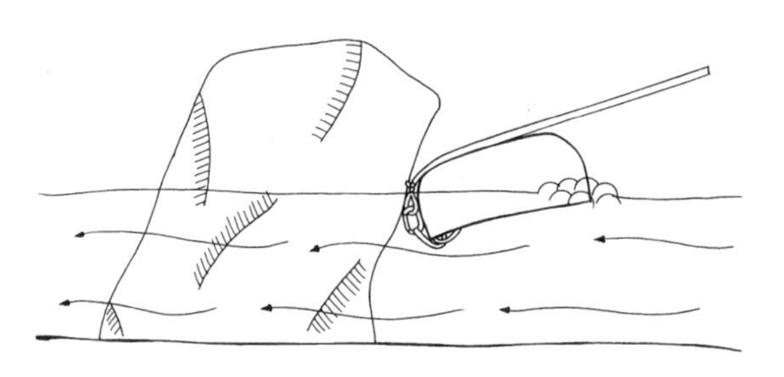

The canoe is no longer held in place by the friction of the hull against the obstacle. The canoe will rotate another 180° and come to rest the right way up. The current may now push the canoe around the obstacle, or it can be pulled free manually.

best passed over the high side to your pulling point (p. 108). When you apply your pull, the canoe is rolled away from the obstacle, freeing it from the pin. More commonly, the trapped canoe is vertical or has the high side tilted towards the downstream direction, and the rope should be passed underneath the canoe (p. 109). When the pull is applied, the lower side of the canoe is pulled away from the obstacle. This allows the current to get underneath the canoe, between the hull and the obstacle, helping to lift the canoe up and away from the pin.

Both of these methods depend on you being able to apply a pulling pressure which is equal to or greater than the force of the current against the surface area of the canoe. As your pulling force increases, it reduces the pressure of the hull against the obstacle, thus reducing friction and allowing the canoe to be pulled free, perhaps with a second rope.

If there are no easily available points of attachment on the canoe, you may have to use a bridle system to tie the rope on. Use two small loops, one over each end of the canoe and tie them together. These small loops will then provide secure pulling points until the canoe becomes very severely deformed.

Attachment of the rope to the canoe should always be done by means of a carabiner and a sling. These are much easier to use than knots especially if you have to reach down into the water. There is also the danger that the canoe may shift during the recovery, causing the attachment point to now be a metre or so underwater where it may be impossible to undo a knot, especially after it has been loaded.

Once you have the canoe attached to the pulling rope, you must determine the best angle at which to apply the pull. You can't pull directly against the current, because once the canoe comes free it will simply be hanging,

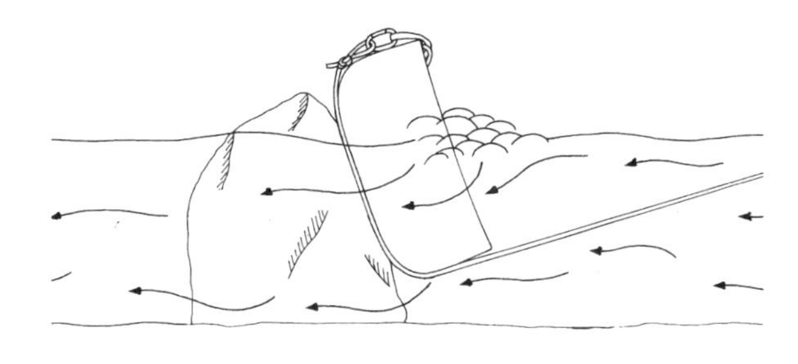

When the high side of the canoe is tilted downstream, attach the rope so that it passes under the canoe to your pulling point.

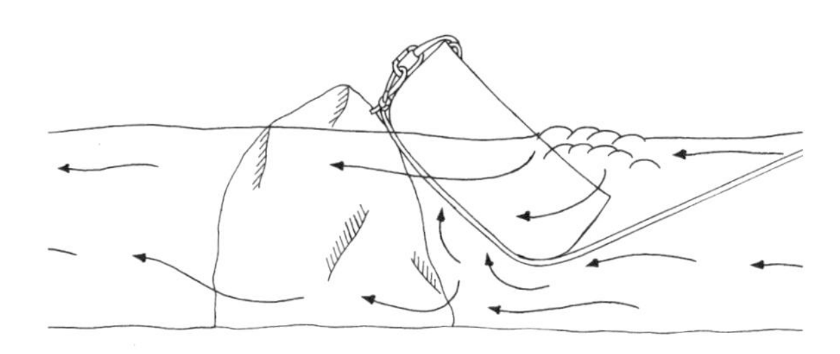

When the pull is applied, the lower side of the canoe is pulled and lifted away from the obstacle.

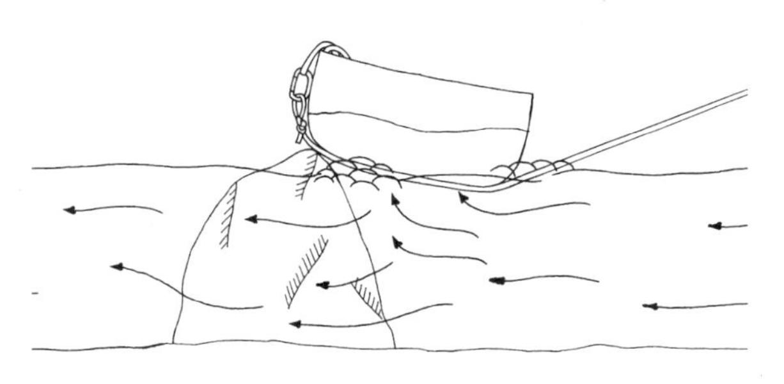

As you pull, the current is allowed to get underneath the canoe, helping to lift it up and away from the pin. The canoe may rotate another 180°, dumping out the water and coming to rest upside down.

effectively pinned on the end of the rope in the current. You also can't pull directly at right angles to the current since the pressure and friction are usually too great. The best angle to pull has to be a compromise between these two extremes. You need to pull against the current to decrease the friction generated by pressure of the hull against the rock, and also pull laterally to move the canoe clear of the obstacle. There is no way to suggest a perfect angle of pull for all situations. It depends too much on the type of obstruction, the exact way the force of the water is pinning the canoe, and the location of suitable pulling anchors. However, a good rule of thumb is to aim for an angle of about 45 degrees between your pulling rope and the direction of the current.

In combination with your main hauling rope, you can also use a lateral rope to help pull the canoe clear of the obstacle. Working in conjunction, two pulling ropes can make a recovery much quicker.

The system you choose to recover your canoe is going to be a combination of whatever equipment you have, and whatever anchor points and accessibility the river provides. The success depends on your ingenuity, on your ability to recognize what the site has to offer, and on your organizational skills.

The pulling rope should be set up at about 45 degrees to the direction of the current.

When there are no other attachment points available, the end loops of a bridle system such as this should allow you to attach a rope to the canoe.

A sea anchor, constructed from a bundle of logs, used in conjunction with an upstream Z-drag to recover a broached canoe. You must be ready with a method to release, or cut loose, the sea anchor once the canoe comes free.

Slings and carabiners being used to attach a pulling rope to a broached canoe in conditions where tying knots would be too cumbersome.

To distribute the load as much as possible, the rope must then pass around the hull of the canoe.

6

First Aid & Evacuation

During an accident, the victim may have suffered physical injuries or may be suffering from hypothermia. The patient's injuries may require immediate or continuing attention. You are unlikely to be very close to skilled medical help, and it is your responsibility to provide competent first aid. In wilderness canoeing, you may have to provide life saving emergency care, and continue your care until the injured paddler can be reached by outside rescuers.

First Aid

The ability to deal with medical problems resulting from an accident is essential if you canoe in remote wilderness areas or on rivers and lakes away from emergency medical services.

While canoeing accidents can produce the whole range of patient injuries, there are few first aid problems that are unique to canoeing. You must always be prepared for the worst when you are dealing with accidents involving water based activities. During a rescue you may be dealing with victims whose injuries are extreme, who may have drowned, and who may require immediate resuscitation. Most medical conditions require the same skills and treatments regardless of whether you are canoeing, hiking, climbing, biking, or skiing.

In any incident where someone is injured or incapacitated, the average rescuer is likely to have feelings of extreme fear, apprehension, and helplessness. This is when experience, training, and practice pay off. Training and practice can help you to cope with the emotional stress, as well as provide the confidence necessary to deal successfully with the emergency situation.

The need to provide first aid can be very distracting for the rescue leader in the stressful, emotionally charged atmosphere of an emergency scene, especially when the rescue of other victims is still in progress. Ideally someone else should be designated to look after retrieved victims until everyone involved is safe.

In a rescue, first aid is not your top priority. Your first priorities in any rescue are **always** to **protect yourself, protect the rest of the party, and protect the patient.** Only then should you proceed with any first aid treatment.

The most important first aid skills for anyone involved in water activities to learn are how to provide Artificial Respiration, the treatment of cardiac arrest, and how to deal with Hypothermia, Unconsciousness, and Bleeding.

First Aid Books

If you are an active canoeist, and find yourself often away from normal emergency medical services, I highly recommend that you enrol in an advanced (preferably wilderness oriented) first aid course. This is the only way to gain the kind of practical, hands on training that is necessary if you are to have the confidence to deal with emergency medical problems. However, first aid skills also require constant practice if you are going to be able to provide useful care after an accident. There are some excellent books available which can help confirm a failing memory, and also provide handy reference. Three books that I recommend are:

Medicine for Mountaineering, 3rd Edition, edited by James Wilkerson, M.D., published by The Mountaineers, Seattle, WA.

Medicine for the Backcountry, by Buck Tilton and Frank Hubbell, published by ICS Books Inc, Merrillville, IN.

Far From Help, by Peter Steele, M.D., published by Cloudcap, Seattle, 1991.

All of these books are directed at the rescuer who is trying to provide first aid in the remote setting of a wilderness accident.

First Aid Kit

A first aid kit is your basic tool for providing emergency medical care. To be of any use, your first aid kit has to be with you at all times. This means that while the first aid kit should be as complete as possible, it must also be kept as small as possible, or else you will be tempted to leave it at home. I recommend that you use a strong, rigid container to hold your first aid supplies. Most first aid items are packaged in sterile paper wrappings which keep the contents sterile only as long as the packaging material stays dry, and is not torn or damaged. If your first aid kit is like mine, it will live in your canoe pack, your backpack, in your bicycle panniers, and your ski pack. It will bounce around the bottom of a canoe, be stepped on, sat on, and have everything piled on top of it. Under these conditions a soft container such as a nylon stuff sac is not sufficient protection for your first aid supplies. I use a plastic "Tupperware" style container, measuring 12x12x20 cm. For list of the recommended contents of a first aid kit see page 122.

Artificial Respiration

Suffocation and drowning will probably be the most serious, immediately life threatening condition you will ever be faced with in a canoeing accident. The treatment for a drowning victim who has stopped breathing is the administration of AR (artificial respiration). AR can usually be initiated without delay in almost any position or location. It can be administered from a canoe, or while swimming or standing in the water, or with the victim on his back, pulled across the deck of a closed canoe. It is of critical importance that AR be instituted as soon as possible, hopefully as soon as the victim's face is clear of the water, to prevent a patient who may be in a condition of quite treatable respiratory arrest from deteriorating to a condition of much less treatable cardiac arrest. AR is a proven life saving procedure, and is what will keep the patient alive if administered quickly. We once performed AR on a girl for two hours until we were able to reach medical assistance. She recovered will no ill effects whatsoever.

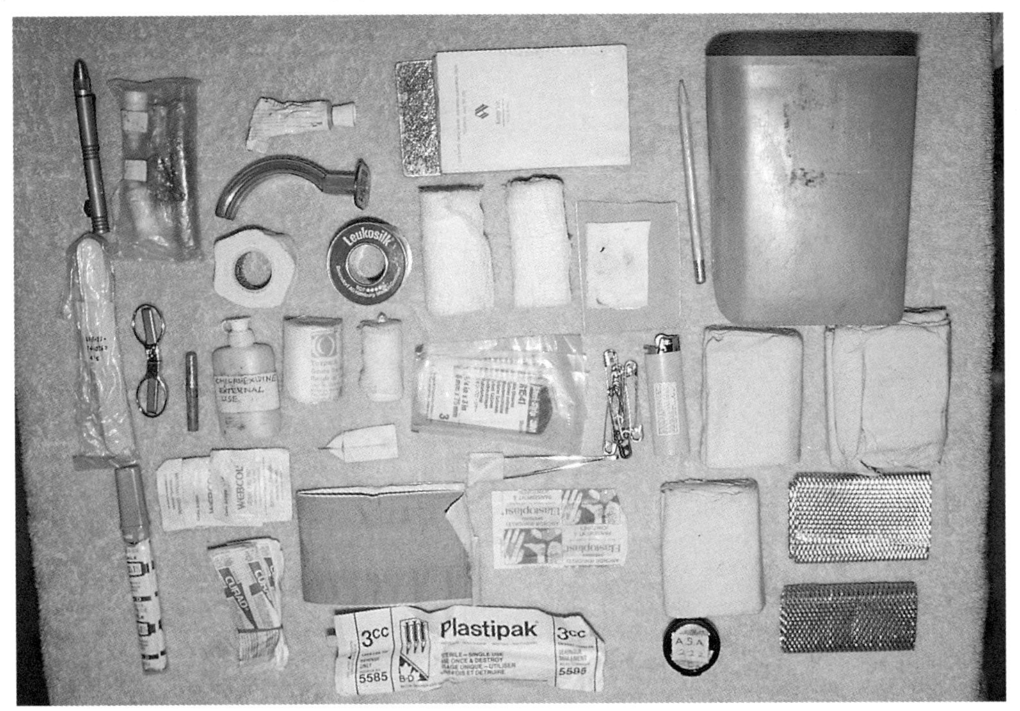

A first aid kit must be as complete, and as small as possible so it will be with you all the time.

Carrying a Pocket Mask for Performing Artificial Respiration

For people who are active around the water, it may be useful to carry a pocket mask, which is a helpful device for administering AR, in your first aid kit. A pocket mask is a clear plastic mask with a soft rubber cuff, and a single port for blowing into. Performing standard mouth-to-mouth resuscitation for any length of time is tiring and uncomfortable, but a pocket mask makes it much easier. It allows you to provide a better seal around the nose and mouth, and has a small one-way valve to protect the rescuer from any secretions, blood, or vomitus that may be in the patient's mouth. The mask is placed over the patient's mouth and nose, and held in position with both hands pulling on the angles of the jaw, and pressing down on the mask. These devices are simple to use and are available through most first aid supply companies for about ten dollars.

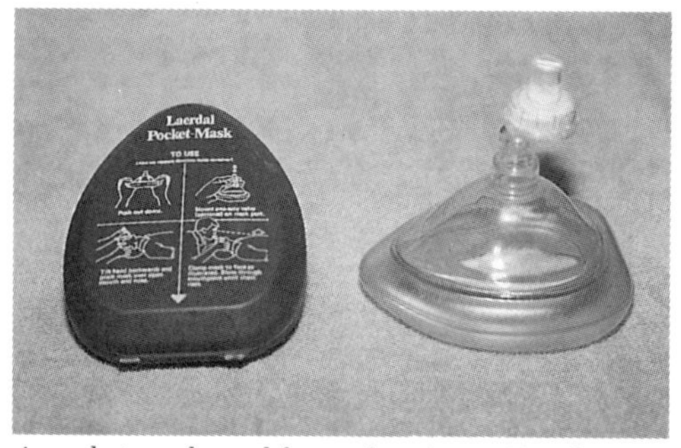

A pocket mask used for performing artificial respiration on a non-breathing patient.

Using a pocket mask to administer artificial respiration.

Performing Cardiopulmonary Resuscitation (CPR)

If respiratory arrest is not treated immediately, it will rapidly be followed by cardiac arrest. Cardiac arrest requires the immediate administration of CPR. However, CPR cannot be properly performed until the patient is out of the water and on a firm horizontal surface. While the administration of AR can be done with the patient in almost any position, premature attempts at initiating CPR are a waste of time. Unfortunately, CPR alone is very rarely a life saving treatment. What CPR does is slow down the rate of brain death, in the hope of gaining enough time to get the patient to a medical facility or ambulance service where he can receive advanced life support treatment.

No CPR course will ever provide you with firm guidelines on when to discontinue resuscitation attempts in a remote area. This is a decision that the rescue leader will have to make. My personal general rule for dealing with this decision in a remote area is, if there have been no signs of life whatsoever after one hour of CPR (no pulse and no respirations) the patient is not going to recover, and resuscitation attempts should be discontinued. If this is a problem that concerns you, you should go and discuss the matter with your own family doctor or local emergency physician.

CPR must performed on a firm, horizontal surface. The PFD has been opened to allow proper "landmarking" and hand positioning on the victim's chest.

Hypothermia

Hypothermia is one the most common serious and truly life threatening medical conditions that occurs during canoeing activities. It is a condition where the body core temperature drops to less than 35°C as a result of immersion in cold water, or from becoming wet and cold while paddling.

As the body temperature drops, very complex metabolic, chemical, and physical changes take place. Unless the process is halted and reversed by outside intervention, the patient's level of consciousness decreases until he passes into a coma and dies. The development of hypothermia progresses through a predictable sequence of symptoms. If it is not stopped in time, the condition becomes irreversible and the victim will die regardless of your interventions.

When a person's body temperature begins to drop, they show all the normal signs of being cold. There is shivering, and an increased sensation of cold. As the temperature continues to drop, shivering stops and the patient begins to suffer a decreased level of consciousness. The patient becomes lethargic, uncoordinated, and loses the ability to make dependable judgements. As the condition worsens, the patient becomes completely unconscious. Eventually the patient suffers from respiratory or cardiac arrest and dies. A patient who has been partially or entirely submerged in cold water for any length of time, may rapidly reach the unresponsive stage with no apparent intermediate symptoms.

Rapid detection of developing hypothermia is the key to successful treatment of this condition. Hypothermia must be arrested and reversed as early in the progression as possible. This means that you should always be aware, and be continuously monitoring the physical and mental condition of the members of your group. If someone shows signs of hypothermia, the treatment is to get the patient out of adverse weather conditions, take off any wet clothing, dry the patient, insulate him in dry clothing or a sleeping bag, and do your best to add external heat. External heat can be added by having another rescuer inside the sleeping bag with the victim, or by hot packs applied to the groin, armpits and stomach. Hot packs can be made by soaking cloth in hot water, then sealing it in a plastic bag. The cloth can be re-soaked at intervals to keep the patient warm. If you can provide this care in the early stages of hypothermia, the patient should fully recover with no ill effects.

A patient who has become unconscious as a result of hypothermia, is very difficult to assess and treat correctly. When a patient is unconscious from hypothermia, and their skin is very cold and moist, and your hands are very cold and moist, it can be extremely difficult to detect a pulse. Detection is made difficult because the hypothermic patient may already have a very weak and slow pulse. I recommend that you take at least a full minute to check for a pulse in a hypothermic patient; the 7-12 second pulse check recommended when you take CPR courses is insufficient in hypothermia situations. There are two reasons for checking carefully for any sign of a pulse. Firstly, if any pulse is present, even one that is very weak and slow, it is probably going to produce far better circulation than any CPR you could perform. Secondly, if CPR is initiated on a cold heart when there is a weak pulse present, it could irritate the heart and actually cause cardiac arrest. Remember that any rough handling of a severely hypothermic patient may irritate the heart and produce cardiac arrest. Severely hypothermic patients must be treated very gently at all times.

There are few guide lines available for treating severely hypothermic patients in remote areas. Providing basic first aid support is the best thing that the rescuer can do, because these patients require the facilities of a well equipped hospital for proper treatment.

When faced with a patient who is unconscious from severe hypothermia, the on scene rescuer should, first and foremost, treat the patient very gently, keeping him as still as possible at all times. If after very careful assessment, the patient is found to be pulseless and non-breathing, CPR should be initiated. The patient should be protected from the cold exposure, preferably in a shelter such as a tent which can be heated to provide a warm environment. You can then prevent further heat loss and try to keep the patient warm by any of the previously described methods. Anyone suffering from moderate or severe hypothermia should be transported to appropriate medical facilities as soon as possible.

Dealing With an Unconscious Patient

Unconsciousness is always considered to be a medical emergency regardless of the cause. Dealing with an unconscious patient, whether from near drowning, hypothermia, or from injuries or shock, is a priority first aid task. While the cause of the unconsciousness is an important consideration, there may be little the rescuer can actually do about it. One of the most common causes of death in unconscious patients is aspiration; getting foreign material, such as food, water, blood and even the tongue, into the very back of the throat where it blocks the passage of air into the lungs resulting in suffocation. This is a situation where the first aider can really make a difference in the survival of the patient. In order to prevent aspiration, you should instruct one person to monitor the unconscious patient continuously to ensure that the airway remains open. This is probably the most important treatment that you can perform for any unconscious patient. From the time you lay your hands on the victim, throughout the rescue, and during the evacuation, one person should be doing absolutely nothing else but monitoring the unconscious victim's airway and breathing.

The Recovery Position

If you are alone, you must still deal with the problem of controlling the patient's airway. This is best done by putting the patient in the recovery position; three quarters prone. This position prevents the tongue from falling back and blocking the airway, allows the best drainage of the airway should the patient vomit while he is unattended, and also allows any blood or secretions to drain away from the back of the throat. Placing the patient in the recovery position does not remove your responsibility for continuously monitoring the patient whenever possible. An unconscious patient should never ever be positioned on their back while unattended.

Dealing with Blood Loss

If a victim suffers lacerations during an accident, from debris in the water or from damaged equipment, blood loss can be severe. Blood loss, if not arrested and treated leads to shock, and possibly death. Patients who are in the water for any length of time can lose large amounts of blood which is immediately washed away. The water also prevents the blood from clotting and therefore bleeding continues. For the rescuer, it may be impossible to estimate the amount of blood lost because of the lack of evidence. It is imperative to examine the patient thoroughly to locate all wounds, as well as treating for shock even though there may be little physical evidence of blood loss.

Paddlers often suffer from other less serious lacerations and abrasions especially about the hands, both from canoeing accidents, and accidents around the campsite. While these injuries may not be severe, it is difficult for canoeists to keep them dry so that they can heal quickly and properly, and to protect them from infection. There are a couple of ways to help solve this problem. One is to carry Friars Balsam, also known as Tincture of Benzoin, in your first aid kit. This is a sticky liquid that is applied to the skin, and helps to hold tape in place, even when the skin gets wet. Another is to use rubber gloves over your bandages to help keep them dry and allow the wounds to heal cleanly. Surgical gloves, latex examining gloves, or even dishwashing rubber gloves can be used, but should be removed whenever possible to prevent infection developing in the warm, damp environment inside the glove. If your hands are going to get right into the water, some tape around the cuff end of the glove will prevent any water from getting inside. A regular glove or mitt worn overtop will protect the latex glove from abrasion and damage.

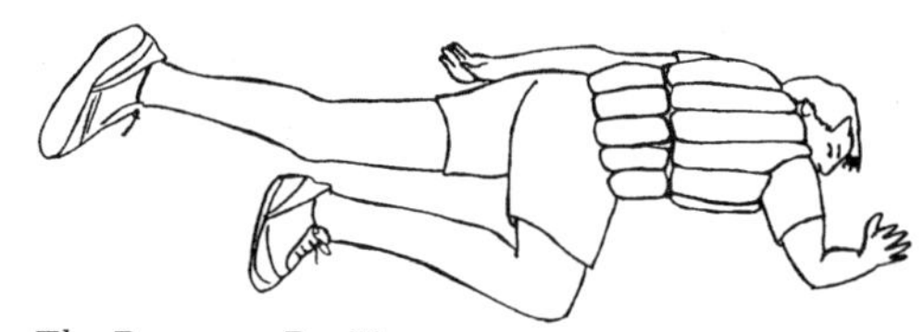

The Recovery Position

Evacuating the Victim

If a victim requires care beyond first aid after an accident, the rescue is not complete until they are evacuated and turned over to professional medical personnel. A major decision in any rescue is whether to stay in place and wait for help, or try to get the victim out as far as possible on your own. If conditions permit and you have supplies and equipment, it is usually best to stay where you are and send for help. Transporting an injured patient over rough terrain is far more difficult that most people can imagine.

Because of the difficulties and hazards involved in moving injured victims and navigating a rescue party across rough terrain, once you have the victim on shore in a reasonably protected site, it is usually more prudent to establish yourself as best you can, and send for help. Staying where you are usually provides the best chance of a successful rescue. It reduces the chances of further injury to the patient or to the rescuers, makes it easier to continually provide care for an injured patient, requires the least amount of resources, and usually makes it easier for outside rescuers to locate you.

Sending for Help

The first step in evacuation is to send for help. How this is done depends on where the accident happens. The important consideration is to ensure that you convey **all** the necessary information to the nearest response organization. If you are sending a person out to get help, they should be carrying a map with the exact location of your party clearly marked, and a detailed indication of your proposed route if you intend to move. They should also carry a complete record of the condition and injuries of all victims, as well as your assessment of what supplies and support you will need. This should include your assessment of the accessibility of the accident site, and what would be the best mode of transport in your situation, such as helicopter, fixed wing aircraft, ground vehicle, or powerboat.

Whenever possible, you should never send just one person to get help. If that person happens to get into trouble, your help may never arrive. The party you send for help should be as strong as your resources allow without dangerously weakening the group left behind.

Remaining at the Accident Site

Once you have established a camp, the next step is to ensure that you can be found by the incoming searchers. It is important to have some signalling system in place to assist any rescuers who may be looking for you. An EPIRB goes a long way to solving this problem. A smoky fire is another good way to signal to searchers both on the ground and in the air. Your other handy devices for this purpose are metal signalling mirrors, and flare guns. Both of these devices can work very well, but they both have disadvantages which are a function of environmental conditions. You need sunlight for a signalling mirror to work, and flare guns are not easily seen from any distance in bright sunlight. These devices at least compliment each other, and between the two of them, you should be able to produce a useful signal.

Paddlers should also be familiar with the standard ground to air communication signals (see page 124). These signals can be stamped out in sand, snow, or constructed out of branches or stones. When you are trying to communicate with a circling aircraft, these ground signals should be large, the bigger the better.

Transporting an Injured Patient in a Canoe

A decision to transport an injured victim by canoe must be weighed very carefully. A patient who is injured and cannot swim, or cannot fend for himself in the water, should never be transported by canoe if there is the least chance that a capsize could occur. Taking such a person in a canoe should be viewed as a last resort. It should only be considered if your resources and the condition of the patient make it impossible to wait for help.

If you must transport a patient by canoe, special precautions should be taken to paddle a very conservative route and to keep your safety margin as wide as possible. The canoe should have the maximum amount of freeboard, and this means that no extra baggage should be in the canoe. If a patient is carried lying flat in a canoe, the midship thwart at least should be removed. This allows for easy access in loading and unloading the patient, and will give you the best possible chance of saving the patient should the canoe capsize. If the conditions are less than perfect, you may need a more stable platform than a single canoe can provide. Such a platform can be constructed as previously described, by firmly lashing two canoes together. With two or three more saplings lengthwise between the canoes, the patient can lie on top of the platform. A platform such as this can be paddled without too much difficulty for short distances.

Carrying a Stretcher in Rough Terrain

It is not practical to attempt to carry a stretcher over long distances in rough terrain, and with the availability of helicopter rescue and modern slinging techniques it is not usually necessary. Carrying a stretcher should be limited to transporting the patient to a safe and accessible location for pickup.

In order to carry a stretcher any distance over rough terrain requires at least seven people. Six to carry the litter, and one to direct the operation and find the best route. Ropes and lowering systems can be used to assist in stabilizing the stretcher when negotiating any steep slopes, in case one of the carriers should slip. They must not be used as a primary means of support unless they are made for the purpose (mountaineering or rescue ropes) and the rescuers are appropriately trained. Moving a stretcher over rough obstacles such as logs, boulders, or ditches and gullies, is a two phase operation. First, with one person only directing the movements, the carriers keep their feet still, and pass the stretcher along until it is fully supported and held by the four forward carriers. The last two carriers then let go and move around to the front end of the stretcher and get firmly set into position. The stretcher is then passed forward again until the four forward carriers have a firm hold. The last two carriers let go and move forward, and the process is continued until the obstacle is passed. In this process the stretcher moves, or the rescuers move, but they do not both move at the same time. Although a slow process, this procedure ensures that the victim will not be dropped.

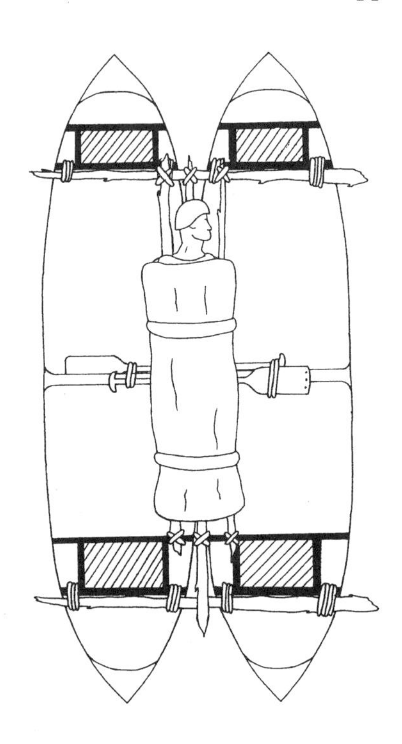

Two canoes tied together to form a raft, with the injured person on a longitudinal central platform. The head is visible to, and accessible to, the stern paddlers.

Legal Considerations

People are always asking me, "What happens if I get sued as a result of my involvement in a canoeing accident?" There seems to be an unnecessarily high degree of public concern over the possibility of legal liability when providing emergency medical aid, and when involved in a rescue. For the most part, there is little need for concern, and the chance of anyone successfully suing you for things that happen during a rescue is slim. I have been paddling for well over twenty years, both recreationally and professionally, in all aspects of the sport. To the best of my knowledge, no one in Canada has ever been successfully sued for providing volunteer help in an emergency. Having said that, I still think it is important for paddlers to understand a little bit about the way the law looks at accidents and rescue.

Emergency Medical Aid Act

If you are a recreational canoeists in a non-professional capacity, you are usually legally protected by some type of "Good Samaritan" law. In Alberta, it is the Emergency Medical Aid Act. In the other provinces and states there are usually similar laws. It is worthwhile to look into the local laws of the area you will be paddling in to see what legislation is in effect. The idea behind these type of laws is to encourage people to help others in trouble, without having the fear of being sued. There are usually two stipulations to these Acts which are worth understanding. The Acts normally state that you are not legally liable for negligence if:

- you have no duty to act,
- you are providing your assistance completely voluntarily with no expectations of reward or payment.

"No duty to act" means that you have no legal requirement to respond to a person in trouble. As a passerby at any accident scene, you as an individual, are in no way legally obligated to offer assistance. Whether or not you are morally obligated to help is between you and your conscience. Professional responders, on the other hand, such as Paramedics, Police, Park Wardens, and Fire-fighters, do have a legal requirement to respond, and therefore are not protected by an Emergency Medical Aid Act.

As long as these two stipulations are met, then you are protected from being sued for negligence in your actions during an emergency.

If, as a volunteer, you offer assistance in any emergency, as long as you act in good faith and with common sense, it will be very difficult for you to be successfully sued for negligence.

One other consideration of note is the concept of "abandonment". This means that if you do choose to assist someone in trouble, you have to keep providing the assistance or you are considered to have "abandoned" the patient. The theory here is that your action in initiating emergency care may have deterred others from offering help.

Professional responders on the other hand, have a specific, legal, duty to respond. This excludes them from the protection of a good samaritan law. This exclusion may also apply to others who have a recognized position of authority as a group leader, such as a canoe instructor, a teacher in charge of a school group, individuals in charge of club outings, or canoe guides. When you are in the position of recognized responsibility, your protection in the law comes from maintenance of standards. This means having appropriate levels of training, and recognized operating procedures. You work within the bounds of your level of training, and follow your recognized procedures. The way the law would judge you is according to the general standard of care in your activity. For canoeing, the standard of care might read as follows: "The paddler is expected to possess that degree of knowledge and skill, and to exercise that degree of care, judgement, and skill which other paddlers of good standing of the same school or system of practice usually exercise in the same or similar localities under like or similar circumstances." This means that as long as your training and procedures are consistent with similar programs elsewhere, and you act within the limits of your training, you should have little difficulty with liability.

First Aid Supplies

The quantity of first aid supplies you carry will depend on the size of your group. The following items are a suggested list of the contents of a first aid kit, for a small group of two or three paddlers.

Description	Size	Number
first aid manual		1
pencil and paper		1
Medications		
Acetylsalicylic acid (ASA)	300 mg	20 tabs
Acetaminophen (Tylenol)	500 mg	20 tabs
Antihistamines (diphenhydramine/benadryl)	50 mg	20 tabs
Gravol (dimenhyrdrinate)	50 mg	20 tabs
Muscle relaxant (Robaxin)	500 mg	20 tabs
Supplies		
bandaids	assorted	10
adhesive tape	2.5 cm	2 rolls
elastoplast bandage	5 cm	1 roll
individual gauze pads	5x5 cm	5
	10x10 cm	5
gauze roller bandages	10 cm wide	2 rolls
triangular bandages	large	3
moleskin		300 sq cm
antiseptic soap/solution	50 ml	1
tincture of benzoin	20 ml	1
aluminum mesh splints		2
scissors		1
tweezers		1
latex rubber gloves		1 pair
plastic oral airway		1
pocket resuscitation mask		1
needle		2
razor blade/scalpel blade		1
eye snare		1
20-50 cc irrigation/suction syringe		1
metal mirror		1

Survival Kit

Some of the items which might be considered for inclusion in a personal survival kit:

matches in a waterproof container or lighter
candle
wire saw
map & compass
fishing line/hooks
emergency food; chocolate, dried soup, beef jerky
aluminum foil
flysheet/space blanket
nylon cord
signal mirror
first aid supplies
water purification tablets
insect repellant

Equipment Checklist

Safety

large plastic bags	2/paddler/week
wet suit/dry suit	1/paddler
neoprene boots	1pr/paddler
survival kit	1/paddler
PFD	1/paddler
painters/end loops	2/canoe
bailer	1/canoe
whistle	1/paddler
maps	2/group
extra clothes in waterproof bag	1/paddler
food & drink	each paddler

Rescue

knife	1/paddler
saw	2/group
rope	1 rescue rope/group
throwbags	1/canoe
slings	1/paddler
prusik loops	1/paddler
carabiners	2/paddler
rescue pulleys	2/group
first aid kit	1/large enough for whole group
rescue beacon	1/group
signal mirror & flare gun	1/group

Standard Ground to Air Communication Signals

What to Do After a Capsize

On Flat Water

1. Hold on to the paddle
2. Hold on to the canoe
3. Assist your Partner
4. Be Aware of Rescue Procedures

In moving water

1. Hold on to the paddle
2. Hold on to the canoe
3. Move to the Upstream End of the Canoe
4. Face Downstream on your Back with Feet on the Surface
5. Assist your Partner
6. Be Aware of Rescue Procedures

Flowchart of the Ten Steps to Rescue

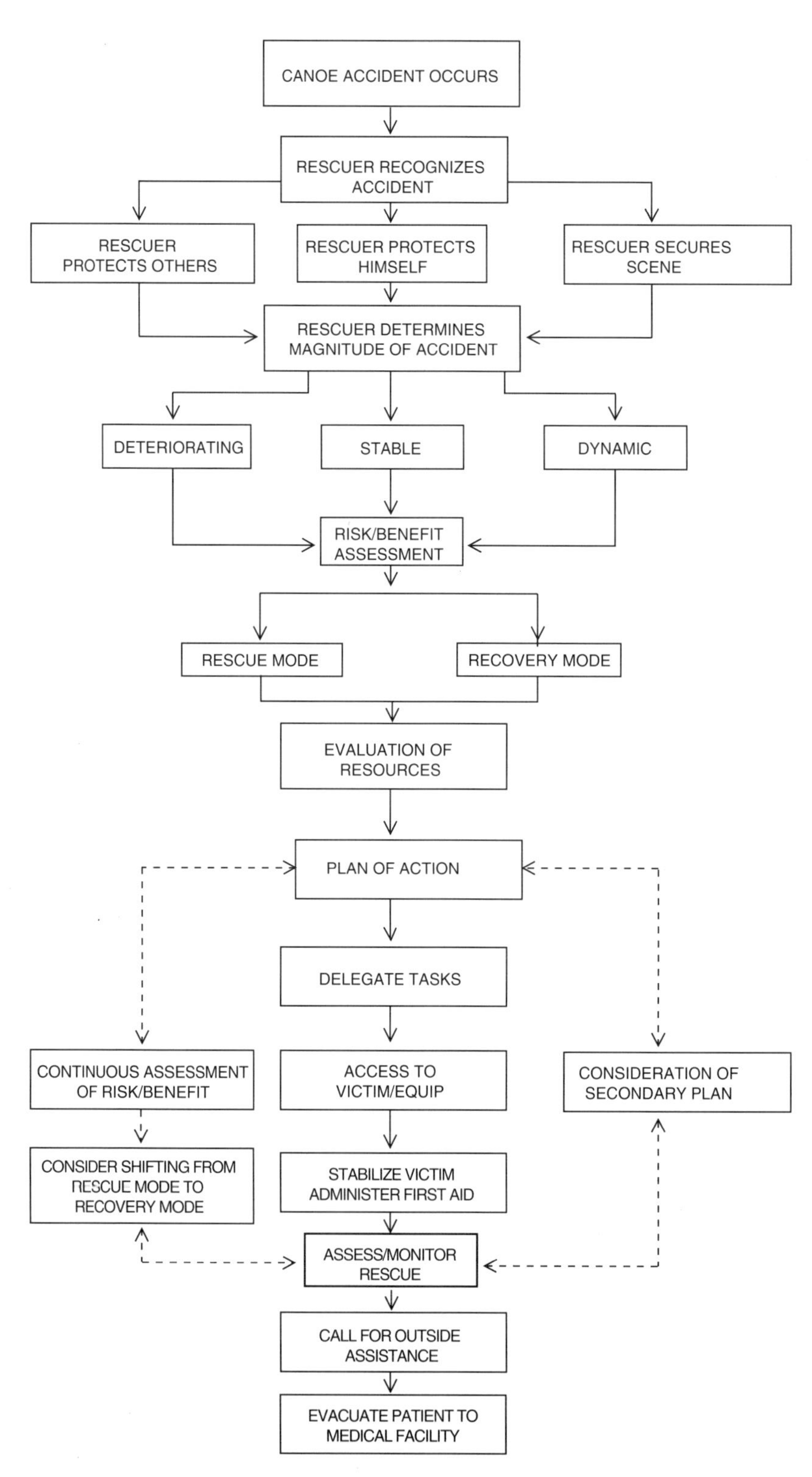

Flowchart for Choosing a Rescue Method

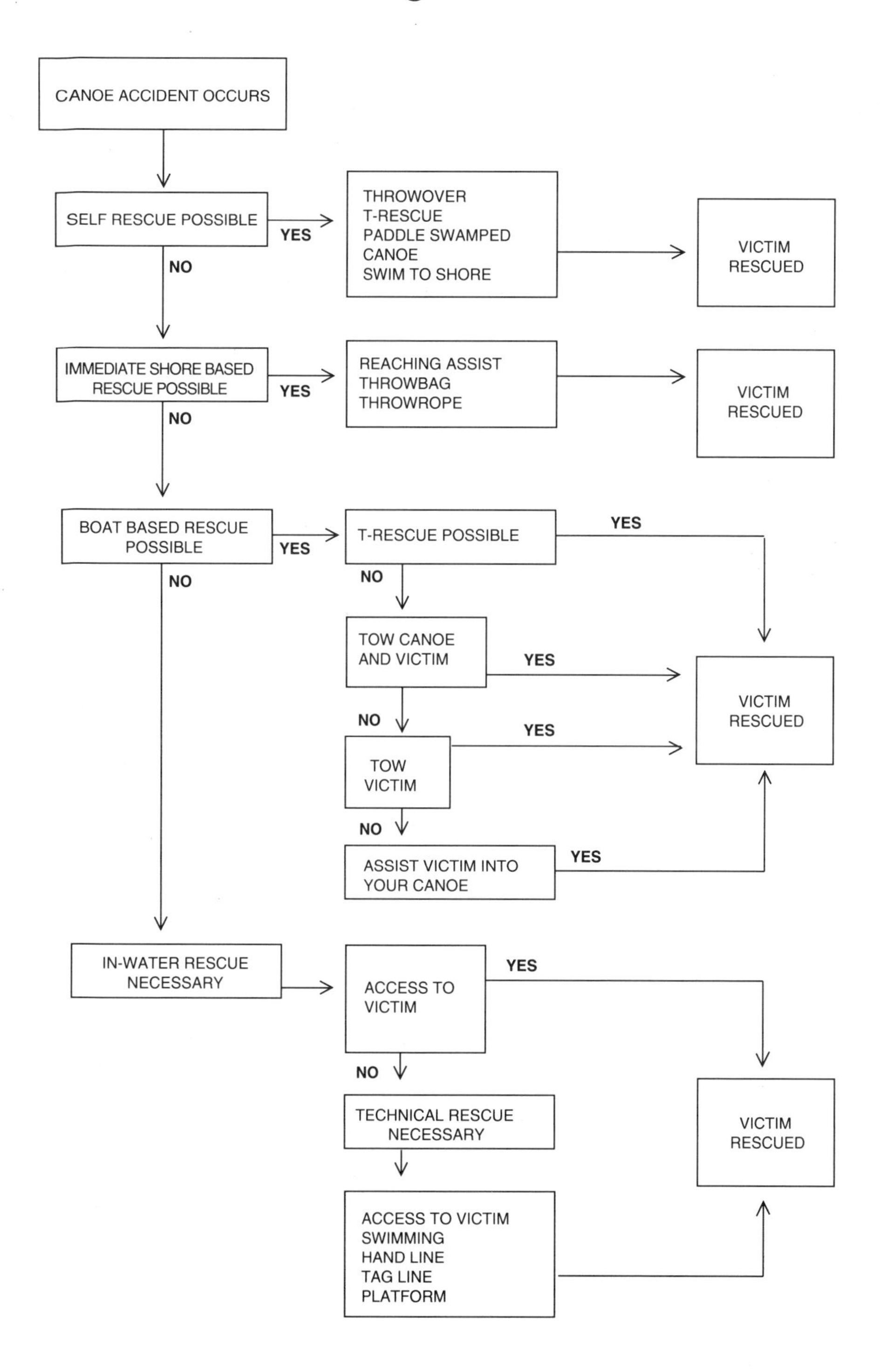

Index

Anchoring a Rope ... 90
Angle Pull ... 99
Artificial Respiration ... 115
  from the Canoe ... 79
Assisting Victim into his Canoe ... 81
  into the Rescuer's Canoe ... 82
  in the Water ... 78
Attaching Rescuer to Lowering Rope ... 105
Audio Signals ... 48
Bailer ... 19
Blood Loss ... 118
Body Belay ... 103
Broached Canoes ... 106
Capsize - skills needed if you ... 61
  what to do after ... 125
Carabiner Friction Wrap ... 104
Carabiners ... 27
Cardiopulmonary Resuscitation ... 116
Carrying Stretcher in Rough Terrain ... 120
Choosing a Rescue Method ... 127
Clove Hitch ... 87
Combining Rescue Techniques ... 83
CPR ... 116
Drysuit ... 12
Eddy Lift ... 107
Emergency Medical Aid Act ... 121
Emptying Canoe ... 68
End Loops ... 23
EPIRB ... 34
Equipment ... 9
  keeping waterproof ... 10
  checklist ... 123
Evacuating the Victim ... 119
Figure Eight Knot ... 86
First Aid ... 113
  books ... 114
  kit ... 27, 115
  supplies ... 122
Fisherman's Knot ... 88
Flare gun ... 18
Flotation - extra in canoe ... 23
  using canoe for ... 64
Footwear ... 13
Friction Hitch ... 104
Friction Wrap ... 104
Getting Into an Empty Canoe ... 69
Ground to Air Communication Signals ... 124
Group Preparation ... 43
Hazards ... 36
  when swimming in rivers ... 65
Headgear ... 13
HELP Position ... 63
Huddle Position ... 64
Hydraulics ... 38
Hypothermia ... 117
Information sources ... 30
Kernmantle rope ... 21
Knife ... 17
Knots ... 86
Legal Considerations ... 121
Loading Canoes ... 49
Log-jams ... 38
Maps ... 32
Marine nylon 21
Mirror ... 18
Munter Hitch ... 104
Nylon Fibre Rope ... 21
Paddling Alone ... 42
Paddling Clothing ... 11
Painters ... 22
Panicking Victim - dealing with ... 80
Pendulum Crossing ... 73
Personal Flotation Device ... 14
Personal Survival Kit ... 16
  contents of kit ... 123
PFD ... 14
Physical Hazards ... 36
Pinned Canoes ... 106
Pocket Mask ... 116
Polypropylene ... 20
Priorities - determining in emergency ... 53
Prusiks ... 87
Psychological preparation ... 52
Pulley Systems ... 100
Pulleys ... 26
Pulling Systems ... 85, 98
Re-Entering Canoe ... 68
Recovery Mode ... 54
Recovery Position ... 118
Remaining at the Accident Site ... 119
Rescue - beacons ... 34
  leader ... 52
  mode ... 54
  plan ... 51, 55
  skills ... 59
  techniques ... 59
Rigging a Rope Across a River ... 92
Rigging Systems ... 85
Righting Canoe ... 68
Risk/Benefit Ratio ... 53
River Crossing ... 72
Rocks and Boulders ... 40
Rope ... 20
  how to carry ... 22
  how to throw a coil ... 70
  pull systems ... 108
  traverse crossing ... 74
Round Turn and Two Half Hitches ... 89
Safe Lake Travel ... 43
Safe River Travel ... 45
Saw ... 27
Sea Anchor Pull ... 107
Sea-Anchor ... 98
Sending for Help ... 119
Signalling ... 47
Signalling Device ... 18
Signals - ground to air ... 124
Slings ... 26
Storing Gear ... 49
Strainers ... 36
Swamped Canoe - how to get to shore ... 66
Swimming across rivers ... 72
  to shore ... 65
T-Rescue ... 75
Tag Line ... 92
Ten Steps to Rescue ... 56
  flowchart ... 126
Throwbags ... 24
  how to use ... 70
Throwing a Coil of Rope ... 70
Towing a Swamped Canoe ... 77
Transporting an Injured Patient in a Canoe ... 120
Unconscious Patient ... 118
Using a Rope Across a River ... 92
Visual Signals ... 48
Wading across rivers ... 72
  with people for support ... 73
  with assistance of a rope ... 73
Water Knot ... 88
Wetsuit ... 11
Whistle ... 18
Working Platform ... 94
Wrap knot ... 89